icons

A Religious Education Programme for 11–14

Mary Jo Martin, RSHM
Anne White
Ann Brook
Paul Gray
Yvonne May
Damian Walmsley

Vision

Responsibilities

Process

Scheme of work and resources

Teacher's Resources

Published by HarperCollins*Publishers* Ltd
77–85 Fulham Palace Road, London W6 8JB

www.**Collins**Education.com
On-line support for schools and colleges

First published 2001

ISBN 0 00 322137 7

Nihil Obstat Fr Anton Cowan, *censor*

Imprimatur Mgr Thomas Egan, V.G.

Westminster, 29th June 2000

The *Nihil Obstat* and *Imprimatur* are a declaration that a book or pamphlet is considered to be free from doctrinal or moral error. It is not implied that those who have granted the *Nihil Obstat* and *Imprimatur* agree with the contents, opinions or statements expressed.

British Library Cataloguing in Publication Data
A catalogue record for this book is available from the British Library

Commissioned by Thomas Allain-Chapman

Project management by Terry Vittachi

Design and layout by Jordan Publishing Design, Salisbury and Ken Vail Graphic Design, Cambridge

Artwork by Tony Forbes

Cover Design by Ken Vail Graphic Design, Cambridge

Cover photograph © Christie's Images Ltd 2000

Printed and bound by Martins the Printers, Berwick-upon-Tweed

LIVING Catholic Bishops' Confer... of England & W... Sharing OUR FAIT... a national project of catechesis & religious education

Foreword

On behalf of the Bishops' Conference, I am very pleased to welcome the publication of *Icons.*

Diocesan RE advisers, teachers and many others from all the dioceses of England and Wales have worked extremely hard in the production of this programme, which forms an important part of the National Project. On behalf of the Bishops' Conference, I thank them for their dedication and perseverance.

At the Low Week 2000 Meeting of the Bishops' Conference of England and Wales, the bishops published a statement on Religious Education in Catholic Schools. In it they said that the primary purpose of classroom religious education in a Catholic school is:

'To draw pupils into a systematic study of the teaching of the Church, the saving mystery of Christ which the Church proclaims.' (para 7)

In undertaking this task, schools will benefit greatly from the provision of good teaching resources. For this reason I welcome *Icons*, for it will help Catholic schools to fulfil these expectations during the critical years of Key Stage Three.

In their statement, the bishops also stated:

'The importance of the teacher of RE cannot be exaggerated. We are most grateful to all those teachers who, week in and week out, have contributed to the religious education of pupils in our schools. We salute the generosity of the teachers who have brought not only a love of their faith to their teaching but also a deep concern for the well-being of every pupil.' (para 12)

I gladly repeat that thanks and express my own encouragement for teachers in their important task.

✝ Vincent Nichols
Archbishop of Birmingham
Chairman
Department of Catholic Education and Formation
6 June 2000

Acknowledgements

The publishers gratefully acknowledge the following for permission to reproduce copyright material. Every effort has been made to trace copyright holders, but in some cases this has proved impossible. The publishers would be happy to hear from any copyright holder that has not been acknowledged. Any omission will be corrected at the very first opportunity.

Extracts from *The Catechism of The Catholic Church.* Reprinted with permission of The Continuum International Publishing Group Limited, London.

Excerpts from the English translation of the *Rite of Marriage* (c) 1969, International Committee on English in the Liturgy, Inc (ICEL); excerpts from the English translation of *The Roman Missal* (c) 1973, ICEL; excerpts from the English translation of *The Ordination of Deacons, Priests and Bishops* (c) 1975, ICEL; excerpts from the English translation of the *Eucharistic Prayer for Masses for Various Needs and Occasions* (c) 1994, ICEL; excerpts from the English translation of the opening prayer and bidding prayers (general intercessions) from *The Order of Christian Funerals* (c) 1985, ICEL; all rights reserved; used with permission; excerpt from *A Thousand Reasons for Living* by Dom Helder Camera, published and (c) 1981 by Darton Longman and Todd Ltd, used with permission of the publishers.

Acknowledgement is due to the International Consultation on English Texts of the *Gloria* and *Apostles' Creed.*

Illustrations

Tony Forbes, Sylvie Poggio Artists' Agency

Religious Education in Catholic Schools

At their Low Week Conference, May 2000, the Catholic Bishops of England and Wales approved the statement *Religious Education in Catholic Schools*. It is 'the fruit of a long period of discussion, public consultation and the symposium on classroom RE which was held in January 2000'. From the statement:

In the life of the Catholic school, religious education plays a central and vital part. At the heart of Catholic education lies the Christian vision of the human person. This vision is expressed and explored in religious education. Therefore, religious education is never simply one subject among many, but the foundation of the entire educational process. The beliefs and values studied in Catholic religious education inspire and draw together every aspect of the life of a Catholic school. We are committed to classroom RE, then, because all pupils have the right to receive an overall education which will enable them, in the light of the faith of the Church, to engage with the deepest questions of life and find reasons for the hope which is within them (1 Peter 3:15). Religious education is, then, the core subject in a Catholic school.

In 1996, we published the *Religious Education Curriculum Directory for Catholic Schools*. This stated clearly the overall aims of classroom RE and its more precise objectives. They can be summarised as stating that religious education in a Catholic school is a comprehensive and systematic study of the mystery of God, of the life and teachings of Jesus Christ, the teachings of his Church, the central beliefs that Catholics hold, the basis for them and the relationship between faith and life; in a manner which encourages investigation and reflection by the pupils, develops the appropriate skills and attitudes, and promotes free, informed and full response to God's call in everyday life. In the words of the *Curriculum Directory*, the outcome of Catholic religious education 'is religiously literate young people who have the knowledge, understanding and skills – appropriate to their age and capacity – to think spiritually, ethically and theologically, and who are aware of the demands of religious commitment in everyday life' (p. 10).

'A Catholic school which promotes the best possible teaching of religious education is fulfilling its true purpose.'

From the Bishops' Statement

The specific contribution to the life of the Catholic school of classroom RE is primarily educational, for its primary purpose is to draw pupils into a systematic study of the teachings of the Church, the saving mystery of Christ which the Church proclaims. Excellence in religious education, then, will be characterised by a clarity of succinct religious learning objectives and of key content, by appropriate methodologies, rigour, richness of resources, achievement of identified outcomes and accurate methods of assessment. Classroom RE will be a challenging educational engagement between the pupil, the teacher and the authentic subject material.

RE teaching in a Catholic school will be enlightened by the faith of the school community and by the faith of the RE teacher. Its educational focus will be formed and enhanced by the vitality of faith. For some in the classroom, religious education may well be received as catechesis, deepening and enhancing their personal faith; for some it will be evangelisation, the first time they will have been presented, personally, with the truths of living faith. Nevertheless, its primary purpose is the step by step study of the mystery of Christ, the teaching of the Church and its application in daily life. The criteria by which it is to be judged are educational.

When classroom RE displays these educational characteristics, then its specific contribution to the life of the Catholic school, which as a whole is a catechetical community, becomes apparent. Then the complementarity of the various roles which contribute to the life of the school is also clarified: the role of the leadership of the school as a catechetical community, the role of the chaplaincy of the school, and the partnership in the religious life of the pupils between the school, the parishes and the families. All these have a part to play in the handing on of faith and its expression and exploration in daily life.

Welcome to Icons

Icons is prepared for Catholic schools in England and Wales at the request of the Bishops' Conference, to implement its *Religious Education Curriculum Directory* (*RECD*, 1996).

The *Catechism of the Catholic Church* is the source and foundation for the *Curriculum Directory* and for *Icons*. Throughout the teacher's notes cross references to the *Catechism* are provided and relevant paragraphs are included in 'For Reflection'. In addition, in each section of work the key doctrinal content is given from the *Catetchism* text.

Icons offers a systematic programme, practical help for classroom teaching and the essential background needed to develop and expand the material to fit the particular needs of different schools and students. It is important for the delivery of curriculum religious education that the principles and vision of the programme are appreciated.

It is out of a shared **VISION** of religious education

that **RESPONSIBILITIES** are identified,

the **PROCESS** is understood and developed

and the most relevant **RESOURCES** are selected and used effectively (see p. 5).

What's in a name?

Icons have a long tradition in Christian art, and are more than art.

They are 'windows into heaven'; 'gateways' for God and to God.

Icons are a profession of faith in the holiness of God the Creator and creation as God's work. (*CCC* 339)

Icons are a profession of faith in the Incarnation. The Word was 'made flesh and came to live among us' (John 1:14). In the human face of Jesus 'we see our God made visible and so are caught up in love of the God we cannot see.' (*CCC* 477–8)

Icons are a profession of faith in Christian belief in God, for whom creation and human life are means of communication and places of encounter. (*CCC* 31–5)

For these reasons, iconographers use only natural materials and prepare for their task with prayer.

In the language of computers also, an 'icon' is a gateway, and the word has come to have a further meaning in speaking of a person who is a role model. The *Catechism* uses it in this sense, describing Mary as 'Icon of the Church' (*CCC* 972), and the ordained minister as an 'icon' of Christ the priest. Speaking of the Christian name that is given to each person in Baptism, the *Catechism* says: 'God calls each one by name. Everyone's name is sacred. The name is the icon of the person. It demands respect as a sign of the dignity of the one who bears it.' (*CCC* 2158)

In all this, religious education can find inspiration. It is a reminder that religious education is about more than the imparting of knowledge. Teachers and students 'open gateways and windows' for one another in the discovery of the gospel that 'speaks' for all time. The dignity of teacher and student is affirmed in recognising that the world and the human person are points of departure for knowing God. (*CCC* 31)

Created in God's image and called to love and know him, the person who seeks God discovers certain ways of coming to know him. These are also called proofs for the existence of God, not in the sense of proofs in the natural sciences, but rather in the sense of 'converging and convincing arguments' which allow us to attain certainty about the truth.

These 'ways' of approaching God from creation have a twofold point of departure: the physical world, and the human person. (*CCC* 31)

Vision

Presents the structure of the programme for Years 7, 8 and 9.

(pp. 4–10)

Responsibilities

sets religious education within the wider context of the Church's teaching tradition and looks at different roles in the religious development of students. Clarity about their role in the classroom enables teachers to select the resources that will engage them and their students in the process to best effect.

(p. 11)

Process

describes the threefold process for religious education in *Icons* – Research, Revelation, Response – and its practical implementation.

(pp. 12–15)

Scheme of work and resources

identifies content to be taught and provides resources:

Learning outcomes

Teaching and learning process

Foundations in key stages 1 and 2

Links to RE Curriculum Directory

Tips for teachers

For reflection

Copymasters

(pp. 16–62)

Icons: the programme

Icons offers a structured, progressive and developmental programme for Years 7, 8 and 9. The structure is shaped by the questions about *Identity*, *Purpose* and *Fulfilment* which the *Catechism* states concern the foundations of human and Christian life. (*CCC* 282)

These questions are addressed and explored in the light of Christian faith in **Jesus Christ**, the **human person**, the **Church** and the ways faith is celebrated, lived and prayed through the **sacraments** and the **liturgical year**.

There are three units for each year. Each includes all the five components: Jesus Christ, the Church, the human person, the sacraments and the liturgical year.

The first and major part of the work of each unit (A) directs the rest of the term's work (B,C,D,E). *Icons* provides for a three term year in which terms two and three vary in length. A flexible component (2/3E) is provided to accommodate this variation.

For each year material for a study of one major world faith is included. This can be studied either as a distinct component or integrated into the year's work.

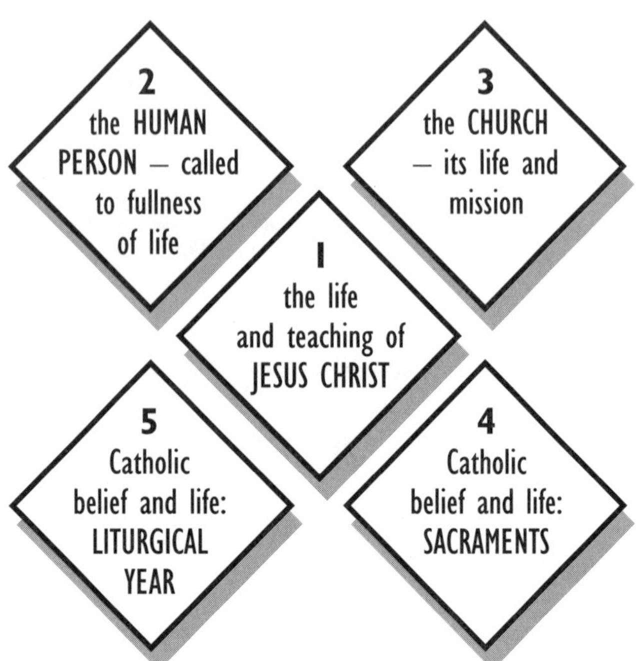

Year 9

Unit 1	FAITH CHALLENGES – human person: icon of God the Spirit (Identity)		
	1A	**To be a pilgrim …**	***Human person***
	1B	Time challenges	*Church*
	1C	Leadership challenges	*Jesus Christ*
	1D	Prayer challenges	*Sacraments*
	1E	Hope challenges	*Liturgical year*
Unit 2	**AT THE HEART OF BELIEF – Jesus: icon of faith and love of the Father (Purpose)**		
	2A	**Word made Flesh**	***Jesus Christ***
	2B	Love	*Church*
	2C	Sacrifice	*Sacraments*
	2D	Resurrection	*Liturgical year*
	2/3E	Something worth living for	*Human person*
		Islam	*Other faiths*
Unit 3	**A VISION FOR LIVING – Church: icon of the Kingdom (Fulfilment)**		
	3A	**The common good**	***Church***
	3B	Living powerful lives	*Liturgical year*
	3C	Living commitment	*Sacraments*
	3D	Living the Gospel	*Jesus Christ*

Year 7

Unit 1	THE LIVING CHURCH – Church: icon of community (Identity)	
1A	**About belonging**	***Church***
1B	A matter of identity	*Jesus Christ*
1C	Living relationships	*Human person*
1D	Celebrating initiation	*Sacraments*
1E	Celebrating Christ's Mass	*Liturgical year*

Unit 2	CHRIST THE LIGHT – Jesus Christ: icon for human life (Purpose)	
2A	**Jesus the Saviour**	***Jesus Christ***
2B	Celebrating Easter	*Liturgical year*
2C	Living as Easter people	*Church*
2D	Called to change	*Sacraments*
2/3E	A place for prayer	*Human person / Jesus Christ*
	Hinduism	*Other faiths*

Unit 3	BECOMING FULLY HUMAN – human person: icon of God the Creator (Fulfilment)	
3A	**Who am I?**	***Human person***
3B	Celebrating Pentecost	*Liturgical year*
3C	Life shared	*Church*
3D	Celebrating life	*Sacraments*

Year 8

Unit 1	LIFE TIMES – Jesus Christ: icon for all times (Identity)	
1A	**In a time and place**	***Jesus Christ***
1B	Making history	*Church*
1C	A sense of vocation	*Human person*
1D	A lifetime's work	*Sacraments*
1E	Future forward	*Liturgical year*

Unit 2	LIVING HISTORY – Church: icon of Jesus Christ (Purpose)	
2A	**The People of God**	***Church***
2B	In search of wholeness	*Sacraments*
2C	Saviour of the world	*Jesus Christ*
2D	People of spirit and truth	*The human person*
2/3E	Churches together	*Liturgical year / Church*
	Judaism	*Other faiths*

Unit 3	HERE IN THIS PLACE – human person: icon of God the Saviour (Fulfilment)	
3A	**A place for everyone**	***Human person***
3B	A sacred place	*Sacraments*
3C	A place for hopes and dreams	*Jesus Christ*
3D	A place for saints	*Liturgical year*

The essential role of theological reflection

If the Church's vision of education is to be implemented faithfully, theological reflection is a crucial part of teachers' understanding, preparation and planning. For *Icons*, this must be a Department activity so that everyone, particularly the non-specialist, is clear and confident about what learning and teaching is involved. Material to support theological and educational reflection is offered for all areas of work (*Scheme of work and resources,* pp. 16–45). These pages are indispensable for the successful use of the programme and offer specific help for practical and reflective preparation.

The material that follows invites reflection on the five major components of the programme. Here, as throughout the programme, the selection offered for reflection is not exhaustive. Heads of Department and others may wish to include material from their own resources and other documents of the Church's teaching – CCRS course material is another useful source.

I
Jesus Christ: Revelation, the Trinity

Theology

Catholic faith proclaims belief in God who takes the initiative in relationship, whose Self-Revelation begins with the gift of life, and whose love is personal and unassailable. This love becomes tangible and visible in Jesus Christ and his unique sacrifice. The Son of God came to live and die for sinners, and his death and resurrection bring new life for all. This new life is poured out for the world by the indwelling presence of the Holy Spirit.

Catechism

The Revelation of God in Jesus Christ, 'since it is the new and definitive Covenant, will never pass away; and no new public revelation is to be expected before the glorious manifestation of our Lord Jesus Christ. Yet even if Revelation is already complete, it has not been made completely explicit; it remains for Christian faith gradually to grasp its full significance over the course of the centuries.' (*CCC* 66)

Experience

In the degree of the truth of our conception of [Jesus] our minds grow broader, deeper and warmer; our hearts grow wiser and kinder; our humour deeper and more tender; we become more aware of the wonder of life; our senses become more sensitive; our sympathies stronger; our capacity for giving and receiving greater … (Caryll Houselander, 1901–1954)

Question

Who/what has shaped my notions of God?

Scripture

The Old and New Testaments proclaim faith in God present, loving, guiding and caring for Israel.

But now thus says the Lord … Do not fear, for I have redeemed you; I have called you by name, you are mine. Should you pass through the waters, I shall be with you; or through rivers, they will not swallow you up. Should you walk through fire, you will not suffer, and the flame will not burn you. For I am Yahweh, your God, the Holy One of Israel, your Saviour.

(Isaiah 43:1–3)

I am with you always; yes, to the end of time.

(Matthew 28:20)

The New Testament reveals Father, Son and Spirit and invites a personal response to Jesus Christ.

God raised this man Jesus to life, and of that we are all witnesses. Now raised to the heights by God's right hand, he has received from the Father the Holy Spirit who was promised, and what you see and hear is the outpouring of that Spirit … For this reason the whole House of Israel can be certain that the Lord and Christ whom God has made is this Jesus whom you crucified.

(Acts 2:32–3, 36)

Who do you say that I am?

(Mark 8:29)

The Creed

I believe in God the Father almighty,
creator of heaven and earth …
I believe in Jesus Christ,
his only Son, our Lord …
I believe in the Holy Spirit …

(from The Apostles' Creed)

Theology

Belief that each one is created in the 'image of God' is the foundation for all that the Church teaches, promotes and defends regarding human dignity, rights, freedom and responsibility. Sin, personal and social, distorts this image. In the Easter Vigil the Church remembers the 'necessary sin of Adam which gained for us so great a redeemer'.

A new creation comes through the Son of God who became human in order that 'human beings might become God' (St Athanasius, AD295–373). By the power of the Holy Spirit, men and women are led to intimacy with God and eternal happiness. This vocation is the root of human need to live in society. It is the basis of moral and social codes of justice and peace and the Christian vocation to love each neighbour as oneself.

Catechism

Catechesis on creation is of major importance. It concerns the very foundation of human and Christian life: for it makes explicit the response of the Christian faith to the basic question that men [and women] of all times have asked themselves: 'Where do we come from?' 'Where are we going?' 'What is our origin?' 'What is our end?' 'Where does everything that exists come from and where is it going?' The two questions, the first about the origin and the second about the end, are inseparable. They are decisive for the meaning and orientation of our life and actions. (*CCC* 282)

Being in the image of God, the human individual possesses the dignity of a *person*, who is not just something, but someone … (*CCC* 357)

2
The human person

Scripture

The Scriptures proclaim human dignity and destiny.

> *When I see the heavens, the work of your hands, the moon and the stars which you arranged, what are we that you should keep us in mind, men and women that you care for us? Yet you have made us little less than gods; and crowned us with glory and honour, gave us power over the works of your hands, put all things under our feet.*
>
> (Psalms 8:3–7)

> *And all of us with our unveiled faces like mirrors reflecting the glory of the Lord, are being transformed into the image that we reflect in brighter and brighter glory; this is the working of the Lord who is the Spirit.*
>
> (2 Corinthians 3:18)

Creed

> *I believe in the communion of saints, the resurrection of the body and the life everlasting.*
>
> (from the Apostles' Creed)

Experience

> *The good news is that you really don't know how great you can be, how much you can love, what you can accomplish and what your potential is. How can you top good news like that?*
>
> (Anne Frank, 1928–1944)

Question

Who and what has developed or diminished my self-respect? What contribution have I been able to make to the dignity, rights, freedom of others?

Scripture

Scripture proclaims the growth and formation of the Church, seeking to live the gospel, united in worship and celebration, confident in God's forgiveness and mercy.

> *Each day, with one heart, they went to the Temple, but met in their houses for the breaking of bread; they shared their goods gladly and generously; they praised God and were looked up to by everyone. Day by day the Lord added to their community those destined to be saved.*
>
> (Acts 2:44–7)

> *In him you, also, when you had heard the word of truth, the gospel of your salvation, and had believed in him, were marked with the seal of the promised Holy Spirit; this is the pledge of our inheritance toward redemption as God's own people, to the praise of his glory.*
>
> (Ephesians 1:13–4)

3, 4, 5
The Church – faith celebrated, lived and prayed through the sacraments and liturgical year

Theology

Catholic belief about the Church is rooted in faith in God as Trinity: the Church is the communion of all peoples, called by the Father, united by Christ and empowered by the Holy Spirit to be the sacrament of communion for the world.

Each sacrament brings about a special relationship with God and with the Church. The sacrament of the Eucharist is the fullest expression of communion with Christ in his offering of himself to the Father.

Christ's life, death and resurrection are the reason for all the Church's celebrations, feasts and seasons. In the Church's liturgy God's loving plan of salvation is revealed and communicated. Christian liturgy has, therefore, a dual dimension: a response in faith and love to the divine blessing, and a continual prayer for the outpouring of the Spirit so that the blessings and gifts of God's love may bear fruit.

Catechism

To reunite all his children, scattered and led astray by sin, the Father willed to call the whole of humanity together into his Son's Church. The Church is the place where humanity must rediscover its unity and salvation. The Church is 'the world reconciled' ...(*CCC* 845)

In the one family of God. 'For if we continue to love one another and to join in praising the Most Holy Trinity – all of us who are sons of God and form one family in Christ – we will be faithful to the deepest vocation of the Church.' (*CCC* 959)

From the beginning until the end of time the whole of God's work is a *blessing*. From the liturgical poem of the first creation to the canticles of the heavenly Jerusalem, the inspired authors proclaim the plan of salvation as one vast divine blessing. (*CCC* 1079)

The Church which is the Body of Christ participates in the offering of her Head. With him, she herself is offered whole and entire. (*CCC* 1368)

Creed

I believe in ...
the holy catholic Church ...
the communion of saints,
the forgiveness of sins ...

(from The Apostles' Creed)

Experience

The church is never a place, but always a people.
The church is you who pray, not where you pray.

(Anon)

Question

What experience do I bring of 'being Church', of praise and worship, of thanksgiving for blessings?

The Catholic school

The RE student

Students live in a world full of conflicting values and a society whose prevailing attitude is that religion, religious belief and practice are irrelevant. They bring to RE many of the values and attitudes of this society, of their families and their experience of Church. Students at key stage 3 are in the process of exploring the values, attitudes and qualities that will guide their adult lives. *Icons* addresses issues, questions and concerns that face them today. Learning to ask questions with confidence is an essential part of education. 'The Church's concern is not simply with the teaching of religious truths. Rather it is in the fostering and nourishing of all that makes for a fully human life.' (Cardinal Basil Hume, *Recapturing the Vision*, 1991) In a Catholic school, the presentation of and clarity about the Christian response to questions should never short-circuit discussion. Precisely by presenting clearly that which is true it should lead to the discovery of possibilities and new horizons.

Curriculum religious education is about the multi-cultural, multi-racial Catholic faith and life in today's multi-cultural, multi-faith society. The Catholic Church calls its members to approach other faiths with respect and to recognise in them signs of God's presence (*Nostrae aetate*, 196). This is not an abstract study, but one that aims at enriching students' own spiritual journey. 'Our approach to other faiths is one of "walking on holy ground".' (Vincent Nichols, 'The Church's Mission in Education in a Multi-faith Society' in *Partners in Mission,* CES and *Briefing*, 1997)

RE teachers

The same principles of good teaching apply to RE as to any other subject. *Icons* offers a programme and schemes of work for Ys 7, 8 and 9 that present learning outcomes, clear content and assessment procedures. The Process offers the experienced teacher flexibility and opportunities for creativity. For the inexperienced teacher, it offers a structured approach that will develop confidence about the Church's teaching and how to present it according to the age and capacity of the students. The *Teaching and Learning Process* for each section of work (pp. 16–46) assists selection by outlining the material offered in the student's book. This indicates clearly the Assessment material. It includes notes and cross references to the *Catechism*. *For reflection* provides material to enable theological reflection to be a key part of departmental preparation. Heads of Department and others will have their own contributions to make to this.

The RE Department

The RE Department, at the heart of the Catholic school, has a twofold role:

- to manage the delivery, teaching and learning of religious education in the school through:
  - clear documentation setting out the vision and direction of RE
  - regular departmental meetings
  - planning the RE curriculum to ensure progression and development
  - offering support and ongoing professional development opportunities for RE teachers
  - ensuring access to good quality resources and evaluating the quality of teaching and learning in RE
- to contribute, in collaboration with the headteacher and school chaplain, to the religious life of the school and students' spiritual and moral development through:
  - offering support and encouragement to staff for this whole school concern
  - providing direction, when necessary, for whole school involvement in the spiritual and religious life of the school
  - offering expertise and support to staff and pupils in areas relating to religious and moral issues.

religious education

engages

facilitates reflection

develops

assesses

encourages

teaches

prepares

informs

measures

challenges

questions

supports

How to use the programme

The *Catechism* begins with the human search for meaning, the Divine Revelation of God who comes to meet us, and the response of faith. (*CCC* 26)

Icons: the process

Religious education is both an 'outward' and 'inward' journey. The former engages students in 'learning *about*'. They acquire knowledge and understanding through study, discussion and reflection. The latter engages students in 'learning *from*'. This leads them into critical reflection on their own experience, appreciation of the Christian story and a dialogue between these two.

The Bishops' *Religious Education Curriculum Directory* presents the curriculum content of religious education. *Icons* is a programme for implementing that content for key stage 3 students. It does this through a three-fold process: **Research, Revelation, Response**. It provides a methodology and structure. It is a teaching and learning process. It engages students in the continuing journey of learning about and learning from the Catholic vision and understanding of life. In this sense, *Icons* aims 'to communicate the rich vision of faith to today's seekers'. (*RECD* p. 6)

The QCA document, *Religious Education Non Statutory Guidance on RE* (QCA/00/576) recognises that there is a variety of starting points and teaching approaches. It describes three teaching and learning approaches: conceptual, ethnographic, human or personal (p. 22). In each it highlights the need to 'identify a key aspect of human or personal experience to create a bridge to the religious concept'.

RESEARCH introduces students to the area of work being studied:

- it raises questions about meaning and what is involved in this study
- it starts from where students are
- it takes aspects of the area of work being studied and links them to students' experience and previous learning
- it invites enquiry and reflection on the area of work being studied
- it offers glimpses of new horizons
- it challenges students to reflect critically on their own experience
- it invites and enables students to begin to look at their own experience in the light of the living witness of the Church
- it leads students into the second part of the process.

REVELATION leads students into the heart of the area of work being studied:

- it deepens their knowledge and understanding of the Word of God as it is welcomed, believed, celebrated, lived and prayed by the Church
- it enables them to reflect on the reality of God in everyday experiences
- it offers them the authentic richness of the Christian story
- it invites, encourages and challenges them to engage in personal dialogue with the Christian message
- it challenges them to appreciate the call to faith in Christ
- it enables students to understand and appreciate, through study of other faiths, the common human quest for meaning, truth and happiness and God at work in human lives.

Note that the terms **Research, Revelation** and **Response** name the process for teachers. The terms are not used in the students' texts.

In the students' texts Response is named:
Making connections: Y7
Links: Y8
Response: Y9

RESPONSE leads students into consolidation and evaluation of their learning:

- it encourages and challenges them to relate faith to life and life to faith
- it provides opportunities for assessment, recording and reporting
- it engages students in a dialogue between their own experience and the Christian story and Tradition
- it offers opportunities for growth and development in learning about and learning from their study
- it invites and provides opportunities for reflection on possible action that might follow learning.

Managing time

Classroom RE 'requires the unequivocal support of the management of every Catholic school. It also requires ten percent of the length of the taught week for each Key Stage of education' (Low Week Statement). *Icons* is written to meet this requirement. For each section of work, allow: **Research** one-quarter of the time; **Revelation** one-half of the time; and **Response** one-quarter of the time. The process allows flexibility. Clarity about the learning outcomes and the process will give teachers the confidence to adapt and select material appropriately in order to meet the different needs of students. Depending on the timetable structure for RE teaching, *Icons* can be managed in the following way.

MODEL 1 (3 lessons a week)

Unit 1 approximately 15 weeks	
A = 12 lessons	B, C, D, E = 8 lessons each
Research 2/3	Research 2
Revelation 7	Revelation 4
Response 2/3	Response 2
Unit 2 approximately 11 weeks	
A = 9 lessons	B, C, D, E = 6 lessons
Research 2	Research 1/2
Revelation 5	Revelation 3/4
Response 2	Response 1
Unit 3 approximately 12 weeks	
A = 10 lessons	B, C, D, E = 6 lessons
Research 2/3	Research 1/2
Revelation 5	Revelation 3/4
Response 2/3	Response 1

MODEL 2 (2 lessons a week)

Unit 1 approximately 15 weeks	
A = 10 lessons	B, C, D, E = 5 lessons each
Research 2	Research 1
Revelation 6	Revelation 3
Response 2	Response 1
Unit 2 approximately 11 weeks	
A = 6 lessons	B, C, D, E = 4 lessons
Research 1/2	Research 1
Revelation 3/4	Revelation 2
Response 1	Response 1
Unit 3 approximately 12 weeks	
A = 6 lessons	B, C, D, E = 4 lessons
Research 1/2	Research 1
Revelation 3/4	Revelation 2
Response 1	Response 1

Planning is essential to the successful use of *Icons.*

Long-term planning (staff Inset days)

1. Read through the Units to be studied (year's work).
2. Check the teachers' pages for additional information.
3. Get a sense and understanding of the flow of the material and direction of the work.
4. Identify how Section A gives direction to B, C, D and E in each Unit.
5. Begin to reflect on how you might teach the Units.

Medium-term planning (before the beginning of each term)

1. Read through the Unit to be studied (term's work).
2. Check the teachers' notes for additional information.
3. Plan out the number of lessons for each part of the Unit, keeping in mind the recommended time allocation and the importance of Section A.
4. Identify how Section A gives focus and direction to the rest of the Unit.
5. Identify what additional resources you will need to teach the Unit.

Short-term planning (at the beginning of each term and each week)

1. Prepare lesson plans for Section A and other sections of the Unit.
2. Identify the learning outcomes for each lesson.
3. Select the teaching strategies and student activities you will use to achieve the learning outcomes.
4. Prepare the assignments and tasks you will use in each lesson and the extended tasks that might be useful.
5. Plan your assessment procedure for ensuring the learning outcomes have been achieved.

Five habits of an effective *Icons* teacher

1. Be clear about how each lesson fits into the **section** and **unit** of work.
2. Know how the **process** works.
3. **Time management** for each part of the process is crucial.
4. Share the **learning outcomes** with your students.
5. **Assess** student learning every lesson.

Assessment in Icons

Assessment lies at the heart of the teaching and learning process. It:

- recognises and values the unique contribution of each student's abilities and aptitudes
- encourages personal commitment to learning and responsibility for one's own learning
- promotes collaborative learning and communication between all involved in a student's education
- measures and provides information about a student's progress and mastery of skills.

In *Icons*, all formal assessment tasks are related to the *Revelation* stage of the process.

A whole class **Diagnostic assessment** is provided either at the beginning of each section of work or at the start of the *Revelation* stage. It enables teachers to identify students' previous learning and, if necessary, to make changes to lesson planning based on what students know or do not know, understand or do not understand, can or cannot do.

Diagnostic assessment
Y7: *Check out what you know*
Y8: *Check your learning*
Y9: *Think back*

For each section of work the following are provided:

Formative, class work: differentiated. It provides information about ongoing progress and development which can be shared with all involved in students' learning. Three levels are offered, from which the teacher will choose the appropriate task to suit each learner:

A. Core: all students will do this
B. Developed: most students will do this
C. Extended: some students will do this.

Formative, homework: either a single homework or an extended exercise.

Summative, classwork: *Testing times* (Y7); *Test* (Y8); *Assessment* (Y9).

This assesses AT1 (see below). Formative assessment tasks assess both AT1 and AT2. Alternatively, departments may wish to draw up their own end of study procedure for measuring student learning.

The Level Descriptors for Attainment Targets for Catholic Schools have been prepared by the National Board of Religious Inspectors and Advisors (Rejoice Publications, September 2000)

Attainment targets, levels and level descriptors

In *Icons* there are two attainment targets (AT):
AT1: Knowledge and understanding of religion: *learning about* religion; knowledge, understanding, ability to evaluate
AT2: Reflection on meaning: *learning from* religion; ability to reflect on meaning.

The tasks and assessment exercises in *Icons* cover both these targets. Attainment levels and level descriptors to help teachers identify student progress and development are provided (p. 15).

Differentiation in Icons

Icons offers teachers one key differentiated task for each component of work in each unit at three levels: core, developed and extended (See above and relevant pages throughout the *Scheme of work and resources* pp. 16–45)

Recording in Icons

Recording and evaluation assist teachers in both planning and teaching. The end of Unit record sheet (p. 63) may be attached to a student's record. *Icons* recognises the school or RE Department will have a policy for recording.

Reporting in Icons

Reporting provides feedback to students. It also informs teachers, parents, governors and diocesan authorities about the content and quality of religious education within the school. *Icons* recognises that the RE Department will follow the school policy for reporting.

Attainment target level descriptors

From *Attainment Levels for Religious Education in Catholic Schools* (NBRIA, September 2000). Levels 4–7 are given below. Departments will need to have access to the NBRIA document and be aware of Levels 1–3 and 8–10.

Level	AT1: Knowledge and understanding of religion: learning *about* religion	AT2: Reflection on meaning: learning *from* religion
Four	Pupils can explain that beliefs, special buildings, language, places and books are features of religion. They can show how religious practice shapes people's lives. They are able to explain the significance of liturgical actions for believers.	Pupils can discuss beliefs and values which influence behaviour. They can recognise that everyone has personal beliefs and values. They are able to ask questions of meaning arising from their own and others' experience. They can identify places and situations which may be conducive to reflection and prayer.
Five	Pupils can demonstrate that there are different types of religious commitment. They are able to recognise that only human beings are 'religious'. They can use some forms of religious language to convey meaning.	Pupils are able to identify some religious and non-religious beliefs and values different from their own. They are able to show that people have different answers to questions of meaning. They can explain how periods of silence and stillness may be used for reflection and prayer.
Six	Pupils are able to identify some religious principles which others follow. They can select appropriate information to support an argument related to religious issues. They are able to explain some religious concepts and can analyse specific religious practices.	Pupils can give reasons for their own religious or non-religious beliefs and values, and explain their significance. They are able to show that questions of meaning have inspired creative work. They are able to recognise that every person has the capacity to be inspired.
Seven	Pupils are able to explain some of the unifying principles of religion. They can apply religious principles and beliefs to issues of social justice and morality. They are able to show the power of symbols within belief systems. They can differentiate between religious and secular world views.	Pupils are able to explore alternative views and possibilities of commitment, including religious commitment. They can demonstrate the importance of the right to choose, and hold religious and non-religious beliefs and values. They are able to recognise that religions seek answers to questions about human existence. They can explain the importance of reflection.

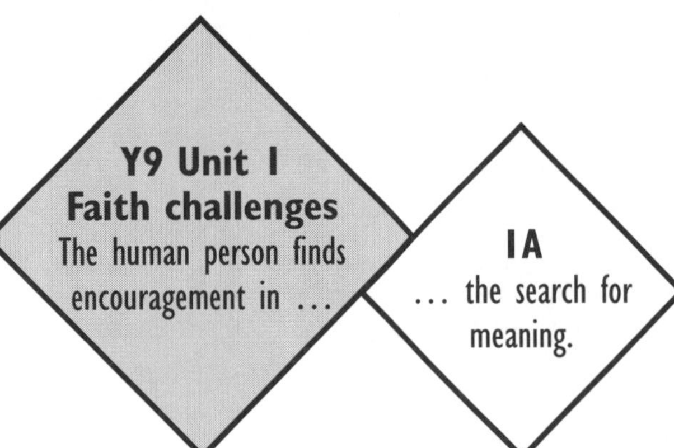

Summary of key learning

Christian life is a **journey** and a **pilgrimage** to God. God calls each one to enter the Kingdom. The **commandments** are gift and sign of the **covenant**, light and strength for the journey.

Teaching and learning process: *learning outcomes*

By the end of this section of work, students should:

- know and understand what it means to be a pilgrim and why people choose to go on pilgrimage
- know and understand Christian belief about life as a pilgrimage, a search for meaning and happiness
- appreciate the commandments (Old and New Testament) as gift, covenant and guide.

Research

Students will have the opportunity to investigate and reflect upon:

- 'pilgrim' and 'pilgrimage' as images for life's journey
- different ways people prepare for pilgrimage and how this concept challenges people today.

Revelation

Students will have the opportunity to learn about and reflect upon:

- some passages from Scripture and Tradition which speak of Christian life as a journey and pilgrimage
- how Scripture presents the commandments: the ten (Old Testament) and the two (New Testament) as gift, light, strength, sign of love and hope for the journey.

Response

Students will evaluate and reflect upon their learning. They will be given opportunities to make connections between their own experience and Revelation. They will:

- be able to evaluate the power of pilgrimage and journey as images of life for today
- demonstrate knowledge and understanding of Christian belief about life as pilgrimage
- demonstrate knowledge and understanding of the commandments for the Christian life journey.

At each stage, select activities to fulfil the learning outcomes.

Research

- (p. 6): starting points: photos, *Paul's story*; why some places are special; the discussion is the way to research (p. 7).
- *First-hand information* (p. 7): interview/presentation skills.
- Evaluate (p. 7): identify key aspects of pilgrimage.
- *Reflect* (p. 7): extension option: research *Pilgrim's Progress*.

Revelation

- *On the way* (p. 8): introduces concept of Christian life as journey with Jesus.
- **Diagnostic assessment:** *Think back* (p. 8): link back to sacraments (Y7, 1D).
- *Pilgrims all* (pp. 8–9): pilgrimage as physical and spiritual; as devotion, spiritual journey, self-discipline. Text from Basil the Great (AD330–370) and Cardinal Basil Hume (1923–1999) develops understanding of and ability to use imagery of journey/pilgrimage.
- *The commandments* (pp. 10–11): focus on commandments as direction for the People of God; code of law; God's gift and sign of the covenant.
- **Formative assessment 1**, *Classwork*: (p. 10).
- Copymaster 1 (p. 10): extension of work with the commandments.
- St Augustine (p. 11): develops concept of spiritual struggle.
- **Formative assessment 2**, *Homework* (p. 11).
- *In light and darkness* (p. 12): links to Augustine's struggle and explores mutual support of Church as disciples/pilgrims (links: to Paul's image of one body, Y7, 3C, and to saving mission of Jesus continued in the Church, St Teresa of Avila's prayer, Y7, p. 46). Group research work.
- Extension option: apply learning for a Year assembly.
- **Elsewhere in *Icons***
  Y9, 2/3E focuses on the Church's belief that Jesus is the Way, the Truth and the Life.

Response *(p. 13)*

- empathy (scripture link)
- question and think deeper (*Reflect*)
- literacy (*Glossary*)
- **Summative assessment** (*Assessment*)
- recognise expressions of faith (*Living faith*)
- extended discussion/essay writing (*Go further*).

Tips for teachers

Resources

A selection of pilgrim guides. For example, to the trenches of World War I, to Iona, Holy Island, Walsingham, St Winnifred's Well, Canterbury.

For teachers:
Free to Believe, 10 steps to faith, Michael Paul Gallagher (DLT, 1987)

Spiritual and moral links

Life is a journey that offers opportunities and challenges.

Additional activities

- Collect copies of some Catholic newspapers and a copy of the annual journal of the National Retreat Association, *Retreats*. Identify places of retreat and prayer in your local neighbourhood or county. Write for information about a retreat house and its programme. Display all the material you receive. Evaluate how they would be suitable for the different Year groups in school.
- Plan and prepare for a class day of pilgrimage or prayer and reflection. What will your theme be? Who will you invite to lead it? Where would it be held and when?
- Find 'Footprints' and use for class or personal reflection.

Doctrinal content

1A: ... the pilgrim Church, in her sacraments and institutions, which belong to this present age, carries the mark of this world which will pass, and she herself takes her place among ... those who await the revelation of the sons of God. (*CCC* 671) The Decalogue ... (describes) for us the paths that lead to the Kingdom of heaven. Sustained by the grace of the Holy Spirit, we tread them step by step, by everyday acts. (*CCC* 1724)

Foundations in Year 8

Students should:

- appreciate the significance of being known by a name
- understand the importance of a sense of vocation for human life
- know and understand Christian belief that God calls (vocation) and how people respond (search, faith and commitment)
- know and understand the significance of the Exodus for the Church.

Links to curriculum directory – KS3

The work in this section relates to the following aspects of the *RECD*. They are revisited and deepened throughout *Icons*. the learning outcomes for this section present the *RECD* for classroom use:

- the Old Testament understanding of life as a gift which requires a response; the Covenant between God and the People of Israel, and the promised land as a symbol of God's faithfulness: – the gift of life is God's covenant with each person; of commitment and response (p. 38, dignity of the human person)
- the commandments as gift and sign of God's love: – the meaning and significance of the commandments that relate to love of God; – the understanding and interpretation of the commandments in the history and tradition of the Church (p. 38, love of God)
- the meaning and significance of the commandments which relate to love of neighbour and self; gospel evidence of how the teaching of Jesus reinforced and developed the commandments of the Old Law; – the commandments and teaching of Jesus are a source of inspiration and positive guidance for Christian social and moral life (p. 38, love of neighbour).

For reflection

Question: Where am I going?

Was the pilgrimage I made to come to my own self, to learn that in times like these and for one like me God will never be plain and out there, but dark rather and inexplicable, as though he were in here?

(R S Thomas)

The commandments were reduced to one by the prophet Amos: 'Seek you me and live.'

(Rabbi Samlai)

Perhaps it is only after the slow slog of searching that one can reach the threshold of Revelation – which is God's love story.

(Michael Gallagher, *Free to Believe*)

Catholic teaching

The term 'pilgrim Church' comes from St Augustine: the Church proceeds on its pilgrim way amidst the persecution of the world and the consolations of God.

Until everything is subject to (Christ), 'until there be realised new heavens and a new earth in which justice dwells, the pilgrim Church in her sacraments and institutions, which belong to this present age, carries the mark of this world which will pass, and she herself takes her place among the creatures which groan and travail yet and await the revelation of the sons of God.' That is why Christians pray, above all in the Eucharist, to hasten Christ's return by saying to him: maranatha! 'Our Lord, Come!' (*CCC* 671)

Pilgrimages evoke our earthly journey toward heaven and are traditionally very special occasions for renewal in prayer. (*CCC* 2691)

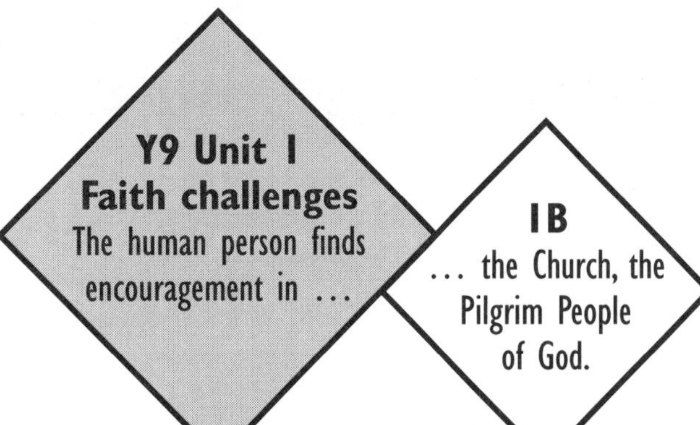

Summary of key learning

The Church is to **proclaim the gospel** through all time and to confront changes and challenges in every age. The **Pilgrim People of God** in responding to these challenges finds inspiration in those who **witness** to their faith in their living and dying.

Teaching and learning process: *learning outcomes*

by the end of this section of work, students should:
- be able to evaluate how people deal with the changes and developments that time brings
- know in broad outline the main changes and challenges that time has brought for the Catholic Church in England and Wales (from the Reformation to the present)
- know and understand why the Church is called 'the Pilgrim People of God'.

Research
Students will have the opportunity to investigate and reflect upon:
- changes: at home, school, in groups and in relationships
- how they coped at the time and how they see the changes now
- what they remember from these times of change and how the memories help them now or might do in the future.

Revelation
Students will have the opportunity to learn about and reflect upon:
- key people, places and events in the history of the Church in England and Wales from the Reformation to the present
- how the Church faced these challenges and why the Church is called the 'Pilgrim People of God'.

Response
Students will evaluate and reflect upon their learning. They will be given opportunities to make connections between their own experience and Revelation. They will:
- have the opportunity to reflect on the challenges of time
- demonstrate knowledge and understanding of some changes and challenges for the Church in England and Wales from the Reformation to the present day
- be able to evaluate the effect of these events for the Church
- demonstrate appreciation of how these are part of the Church's journey as the Pilgrim People of God.

At each stage, select activities to fulfil the learning outcomes.

Research
- (pp. 14–15) Focus on role of time in human life: how people feel, respond, act; time as freeing or constraining. Scenarios offer opportunity for role-play or discussion. Photo images of time may be used as a starting point for students' own 'Images of Time' gallery. Responses may be oral or written work or personal reflection.
- **Diagnostic assessment 1**, *Think back* (p. 16): link to Y8, 1B. Foundations for exploration of the changes the Reformation years brought to the Church.

Revelation
- *Change and challenge* (p. 16): introduce concept of history as change and challenge.
- **Formative assessment 2**, *Homework*: (p. 15): identify attitudes to change.
- History in your pocket (pp.16–7): overview of key people and events of Reformation and post-Reformation in England and Wales. *Copymasters 2* and *3* offer teacher's historical notes. NB, title on coins has not changed, nor has the Act of Settlement been repealed. It forbids an heir to the throne to marry a Catholic or a Catholic to be king or queen. Focus on reversal of the Church's role – visible presence to underground Church and centuries of disenfranchisement.
- *Copymaster 4*: the forty martyrs of England and Wales
  Copymaster 5: source text, words of the martyrs
  Copymaster 6: source texts, last words of the martyrs.
- *Change in the Church* (pp. 18–9); introduce Catholic Reformation and concept of change and renewal in the Church through individuals, Councils and Popes. Class projects (p. 18), opportunity for focused research and class sharing.
- **Formative assessment 1**, *Classwork*: (p. 19)
- Extension option: opportunity to raise current issues that challenge the Church from outside or within.
- **Elsewhere in *Icons***: In Y9, 2/3E, students have the opportunity to explore the Church's challenge to aspects of contemporary cultures.

Response *(p. 20)*
- think wider and deeper (*Reflect*)
- **Summative asessment** (*Assessment*)
- literacy (*Glossary*)
- challenge thinking (*Dilemma*)
- apply scripture to life (*Living faith*)
- for extended discussion/essay writing (*Go further*).

Tips for teachers

Resources

Pitkin Historical Guides.
Local history records and books.
Forty English and Welsh Martrys, Clement Tigar (1961, 1970). Look for library copies.

For teachers:
How to read Church History,Vol 2 (SCM Press)

Spiritual and moral links

People, like situations, change, grow and develop.

Additional activities

- Plan and hold a class debate: "It's the Church today that matters, not what happened all those years ago." Speakers for both sides present their position and then face questions and debate by the rest of the class.
- Links with Y8 work on different Christian Churches. How does this current work help understanding of the causes of division in the Christian family? How might a knowledge of history help the cause of Christian unity?

Doctrinal content

1B: 'The Father ... determined to call together in a holy Church those who should believe in Christ.' This 'family of God' is gradually formed and takes shape during the stages of human history, in keeping with the Father's plan. (*CCC* 759) By her very mission, 'the Church ... travels the same journey as all humanity and shares the same earthly lot with the world: she is to be a leaven and, as it were, the soul of human society in its renewal by Christ and transformation into the family of God.' (*CCC* 854)

Foundations in Year 8

Students should:

- appreciate the significance of family history for personal development
- know and understand the principal events in the history of the Church in England and Wales (early and medieval times) and appreciate their significance for the life of the Church
- know and appreciate diversity and division among the Christian Churches in England and Wales
- know about the week of prayer for Christian Unity.

Links to curriculum directory – KS3

The work in this section relates to the following aspects of the *RECD*. They are revisited and deepened throughout *Icons*. The learning outcomes for this section present the *RECD* for classroom use:

- characteristics of the People of God, in Scripture, in Tradition and in the world of today; the history and development of the Church in Britain … – the Church is a visible and spiritual community; the Church's pastoral role in society; the main developments in the history of the Church in Britain (p. 22 – catholic)
- opportunities for the exercise of freedom and responsibility in family life, the local church and society: at local, national and global levels; – the value the Church places on freedom, responsibility and conscience (p. 38 – freedom, responsibility, conscience).

For reflection

Question: What strategies do I have for managing change?

It is not the pain but the purpose that makes the martyr.
(St Augustine of Hippo)

I have faith because it has been named, articulated, sustained through history by those whom I know to be my companions — that is, fellow human beings who have laid down, however buried in dusty libraries, maps of the land that has to be travelled, so that however dangerous the road, however close to the edge of the chasm I walk, I do have a hint of a path, the possibility of a safety net which will help us all not to fall into the void of insanity or unspeakability.
(Sara Maitland, *A Big-Enough God*)

The tyrant dies and his rule is over; the martyr dies and his rule begins.
(Sören Kierkegaard)

Catholic teaching

It is a feature of the human person that it can attain to real and full humanity only through culture; that is, by cultivating the goods of nature and values. Wherever human life is considered, therefore, nature and culture are very intimately connected. The term 'culture' in general refers to everything by which we perfect and develop our many spiritual and physical endowments; applying ourselves through knowledge and effort to bring the earth within our power; developing ways of behaving and institutions, we make life in society more human, whether in the family or in the civil sphere as a whole; in the course of time we express, share and preserve in our works great spiritual experiences and aspirations to contribute to the progress of many people, even of the whole human race. Human culture thus necessarily takes on an historical and social aspect …

(*The Pastoral Constitution on the Church in the World of Today*, 53)

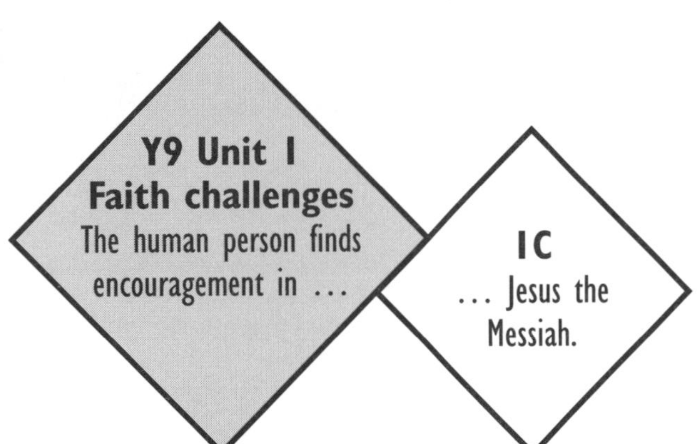

Summary of key learning

The Jewish people looked to the **Messiah** for **leadership**. He would be the One who would deliver them from their enemies and establish God's reign. Jesus, the **Anointed One**, challenged them to go beyond their **expectations** of an earthly kingdom

Teaching and learning process: *learning outcomes*

By the end of this section of work, students should:

- be able to evaluate different styles of leadership in order to appreciate how they influence people
- know about and appreciate some Jewish expectations of the Messiah from evidence in the Old Testament
- know and understand how Jesus is presented as the Messiah in the New Testament.

Research

Students will have the opportunity to investigate and reflect upon:

- inspirational leaders in various areas of life and the kind of leadership people hope for today: school, politics, religion, society
- how a person and his or her style of leadership affect the message, how people hear it and their response.

Revelation

Students will have the opportunity to learn about and reflect upon:

- the concept of Messiah from evidence in the Old Testament
- the New Testament portrayal of Jesus as the fulfilment of people's expectations of the Messiah
- how Jesus in his life, death and resurrection is more than 'a leader' and challenges past and present.

Response

Students will evaluate and reflect upon their learning. They will be given opportunities to make connections between their own experience and Revelation. They will:

- be able to evaluate how styles of leadership affect the message and how it is received
- describe some of the expectations of Messiah in the Old Testament
- demonstrate knowledge and understanding of the New Testament proclamation that Jesus is the longed-for Messiah
- evaluate the extent to which Jesus' style of leadership and his mission challenge people.

At each stage, select activities to fulfil the learning outcomes.

Research

- *Leaders* (p. 21): focus on qualities and responsibilities of leaders and leadership.
  Extension option: apply learning with empathy – design an advert for the job of headteacher.
- **Diagnostic assessment:** *Think back* (p. 21), link to Y8, 1A.

Revelation

- *The Messiah* (p. 22): develops understanding of Jewish expectations of the Messiah (link to Y8, 1D, significance of anointing); source texts from Daniel and Isaiah explore use of imagery.
- *Jesus the Messiah* (pp. 23–4): link back to Mark's presentation of Jesus as the one sent by God and empowered by the Spirit (Y8, 1C) and introduce Matthew's approach relating Old and New Testament sources.
- **Formative assessment 2,** *Homework* (p. 23): focus on how the disciples grew in understanding that Jesus was more than the 'leader' of Jewish expectations.
- **Formative assessment 1,** *Classwork*: (p. 24).
- **Elsewhere in *Icons***: focus on the power of the Holy Spirit and leadership in the spirit of Jesus in Y9, 3B.

Response *(p. 25)*

- think deeper (*Reflect*)
- **Summative assessment** (*Assessment*)
- literacy (*Glossary*)
- question and provoke (*Dilemma*)
- recognising the power of faith to inspire prayer (*Living faith*).

Tips for teachers

Resources

Jesus of Nazareth video (Carlton)
Testament: The Bible in Animation video
In the Footsteps of Christ No 7: You are the Christ – video (St Paul Multi-Media Productions)

For teachers:
Enda Lyons, *Jesus, Self-portrait by God* (Columba Press, 1994)

Spiritual and moral links

Leadership is about service.

Additional activities

- Select clips from videos that portray Jesus, for example, *Jesus of Nazareth, Jesus Christ Superstar, Godspell, The Animated Bible, Storykeepers*. Evaluate the image of Messiah these present in the light of the work completed in class. To what extent do 'modern' presentations help or hinder Jesus' self-presentation in the gospels? Evaluate how suitable the portrayals you have examined are for Y8 students, primary students, adults.
- Identify and discuss what Christian leaders would learn from the example of Jesus in dealing with some of the moral and social issues facing Christian leaders today, for example, the arms trade, the death penalty, legalising drugs.

Doctrinal content

1C: The word 'Christ' comes from the Greek translation of the Hebrew 'Messiah', which means 'anointed'. (*CCC* 436) The one who is anointing is the Father, the one who was anointed is the Son, and he was anointed with the Spirit who is the anointing. His eternal messianic consecration was revealed during the time of his earthly life at the moment of his baptism by John when 'God anointed Jesus of Nazareth with the Holy Spirit and with power', 'that he might be revealed to Israel' as its Messiah. His works and words will manifest him as 'the Holy One of God'. (*CCC* 438)

Foundations in Year 8

Students should:

- appreciate the need for salvation in the world
- appreciate the importance of cultural, social and religious background for people's understanding of themselves and others
- know and understand that Jesus was born, lived and worked within the Jewish faith community of his time
- appreciate the significance of the Passover celebration for Jewish believers.

Links to curriculum directory – KS3

The work in this section relates to the following aspects of the *RECD*. They are revisited and deepened throughout *Icons*. The learning outcomes for this section present the *RECD* for classroom use:

- the concept of Messiah in the Old and New Testament; the life and ministry of Jesus, his teaching, parables and miracles; – the events of the life, death and resurrection of Jesus Christ are at the heart of Catholic faith (p. 17 – Jesus Christ)
- the mission of Jesus as revealed in the New Testament with particular reference to his priestly, prophetic and kingly roles; leadership and authority in Scripture and Tradition and in the life of the Church today; – as priest, prophet and king Jesus proclaims the kingdom of God; the Church's understanding of leadership, authority and service (p. 22 – apostolic).

For reflection

Question: Following and leading? What helps me to keep these in balance?

A suffering Messiah: Jesus did not come to explain away suffering or remove it. He came to fill it with his presence.
(Paul Claudel)

It is wholly in Jesus that the love of God is revealed, a love that goes beyond death.

Catholic teaching

The Messiah's characteristics are revealed above all in the 'Servant songs'. These songs proclaim the meaning of Jesus' Passion, and show how he will pour out the Holy Spirit to give life to the many: not as an outsider, but by embracing our 'form as slave'. Taking our death upon himself he can communicate to us his own Spirit of life. This is why Christ inaugurates the proclamation of the Good News by making his own the words of Isaiah (Luke 4:18–19). (*CCC* 713–4)

In the Old Testament the prophets announced that the Spirit of the Lord would rest on the hoped-for Messiah for his saving mission. The descent of the Holy Spirit on Jesus at his baptism by John was the sign that this was he who was to come, the Messiah, the Son of God. He was conceived of the Holy Spirit; his whole life and his whole mission are carried out in total communion with the Holy Spirit whom the Father gives him 'without measure'. This fullness of the Spirit was not to remain uniquely the Messiah's but was to be communicated to the whole messianic people. (*CCC* 1286–7)

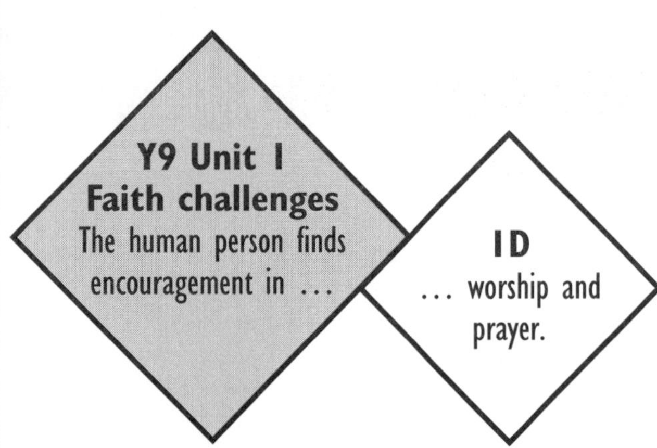

Summary of key learning

People pray in many ways, but all **prayer** is to God the Father **through Christ** in the Holy Spirit. **Liturgy** is 'work of the whole people' in union with Christ. Prayer is **relationship** with the Trinity and both **communal and personal prayer** requires time and space.

Teaching and learning process: *learning outcomes*

By the end of this section of work, students should:

- be able to evaluate people's need for space and time for themselves and for important relationships
- have learned more about the sacred times and spaces the Christian community sets aside for God.

Research

Students will have the opportunity to investigate and reflect upon:

- the time and space people need for themselves and for relationships and why these are important.

Revelation

Students will have the opportunity to learn about and reflect upon:

- how the Christian cycle of feasts and seasons is time for nurturing relationship with God
- formal and informal prayer in Catholic tradition: vocal prayer; meditative prayer; contemplative prayer; types of prayer; liturgical prayer
- the use of symbols in prayer: music; silence; dance; singing; chant.

Response

Students will evaulate and reflect upon their learning. They will be given opportunities to make connections between their own experience and Revelation. They will:

- have an opportunity to reflect on and evaluate their personal times and spaces
- show appreciation and understanding of the sacred times and spaces of the Christian community
- demonstrate knowledge and understanding of some formal and informal styles of prayer in Catholic tradition
- be able to evaluate how the use of symbols can help people to pray.

At each stage, select activities to fulfil the learning outcomes.

Research

- *Copymaster 7* (p. 26): 1B looked at time in terms of change; the focus here is on the pressures that result from different attitudes to time.
- *Targeting time* (p. 26): student profiles; discussion will raise questions of priorities. This lays foundations for the revelation tasks.
- **Diagnostic assessment:** *Think back* (p. 26) assesses work on prayer in Y7, 2/3E and Y8, 3B.

Revelation

- *Through Jesus Christ our Lord* (p. 27) introduces the public, formal prayer of the Church and the main liturgical seasons. Builds on work done in Y7, 1E; focus here is on the changing seasons; opportunities to develop liturgical skills of planning and choosing appropriate texts, prayer and hymns.
- **Formative assessment 1:** *Classwork*: (p. 27) *Copymaster 8*: ***Seasonal prayers and blessings.***
- *Prayer comes from the heart* (pp. 28–9) explores personal prayer and prayer forms: meditation, praise and intercession. Extension option: research Gregorian chant.
- **Formative assessment 2,** *Homework* (p. 29)
- *Prayer time* (p. 29): prayer audit.
- *Icons* (p. 30): a multi-cultural tradition.
- *Aids to prayer* (p. 30): discussion can lead to research on art and artefacts in the school, parish church, local area. Extension option: essay task could be an opportunity for personal reflection.
- **Elsewhere in *Icons***: students will study the liturgy and prayers of Advent and Christmas, Y9, 1E and of the Eucharist, Y9, 2C.

Response *(p. 31)*

- think deeper (*Reflect*)
- literacy (*Glossary*)
- **Summative assessment** (*Assessment*)
- examine different points of view (*Reflect*)
- challenge thinking (*Dilemma*)
- meet Church teaching – *CCC* 2565 (*Living faith*)
- opportunity for extended discussion/essay writing (*Go further*).

Tips for teachers

Resources

Anthologies of prayers: for example, *Prayers in the Celtic Tradition* by David Adam; collections by William Barclay, Michel Quoist: '*Through the year with* ... (St Francis, etc); *Prayers Encircling the World*, an international anthology of 300 contemporary prayers (SPCK, 1998)

For teachers:
Margaret Self, *Taste and See, Adventuring into Prayer* (DLT, 1999)

Spiritual and moral links

All relationships need space, time and special occasions in order to grow.

Additional activities

- Plan and lead an assembly on prayer that will explain and introduce students to the three forms of prayer you have studied: meditation, praise and intercession. Take into account students' responses to your prayer audit (p. 30).
- Research the prayer and pattern of life of a religious community of monks or nuns through the web. For example, *http://www.ampleforthcollege.york.sch.uk* How often do they pray? How do they prepare for prayer? What forms of prayer do they use?
- Read Ecclesiastes 3:1–11. Identify the times when the following people would want to pray: parents who have just had a baby; someone who had just become unemployed; someone whose husband or wife has recently died; a young person leaving home.

Doctrinal content

1D: The Holy Spirit who teaches the Church and recalls to her all that Jesus said also instructs her in the life of prayer, inspiring new expression of the same basic forms of prayer: blessing, intercession, thanksgiving and praise. (*CCC* 2644) There is no other way of Christian prayer than Christ ... The sacred humanity of Jesus is therefore the way by which the Holy Spirit teaches us to pray to God our Father. (*CCC* 2664)

Foundations in Year 8

Students should:

- appreciate the wonder and mystery of being human
- understand the significance of being known by name
- know and understand Jesus' invitation to 'fullness of life'
- understand what it means to say that the Church is 'the communion of saints'
- know and appreciate how the Church celebrates the holiness and example of men and women through the ages.

Links to curriculum directory – KS3

The work in this section relates to the following aspects of the *RECD*. They are revisited and deepened throughout *Icons*. The learning outcomes for this section present the *RECD* for classroom use:

- humanity as created by God; awareness of the transcendent and the holy and of the Presence of God in self, others and the world; – the Church's teaching about human life, dignity and vocation (p. 17 – creation)
- the variety of prayer forms and their significance in Catholic life and history; prayer as God's gift; – variety of approaches to prayer and settings for prayer; (p. 31 – prayer)
- the universal value of some signs and symbols; – the place of universal signs and symbols in the life of the Church (p. 30, sacraments).

For reflection

Question:
Why do I pray?

Prayer isn't a matter of a lot of thinking; it's a lot of loving.
(St Teresa of Avila)

Our prayer is God's work, God's creation. As you kneel there, sit there, walk about or whatever you do when you pray, you are saying 'yes' with your whole being to his will that you should be you, that you should be united to him.
(Maria Boulding)

At this very moment, in all the earth there are Christians, Jews, Muslims, Hindus and Buddhists at prayer. I do not suppose that a single second goes by when there is not a human soul in prayer ... We are not alone. We are a people of tiny quiet flames, burning at night, which get lit from each other and spread through the darkness.
(Petru Dimitriu)

Catholic teaching

'If you knew the gift of God!' The wonder of prayer is revealed beside the well where we come seeking water: there, Christ comes to meet every human being. It is he who first seeks us and asks us for a drink. Jesus thirsts; his asking arises from the depths of God's desire for us. Whether we realise it or not, prayer is the encounter of God's thirst with ours. God thirsts that we may thirst for him. (*CCC* 2560)

The living and true God tirelessly calls each person to that mysterious encounter known as prayer. In prayer the faithful God's initiative of love always comes first; our own first step is always a response. As God gradually reveals himself and reveals us to ourselves, prayer appears as a reciprocal call, a covenant drama. Through words and actions, this drama engages the heart. It unfolds throughout the whole history of salvation. (*CCC* 2567)

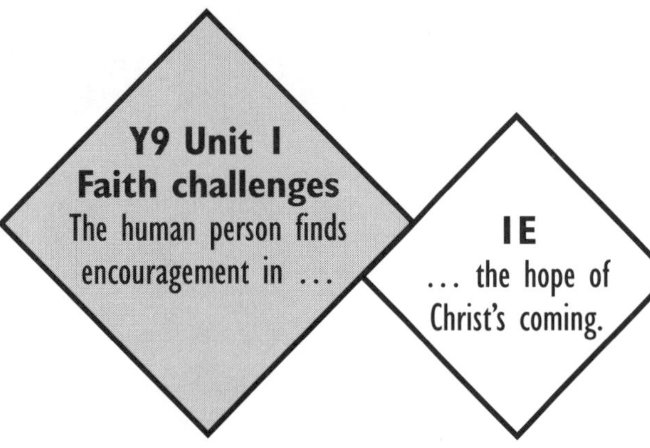

Summary of key learning

Advent celebrates the **expectancy** of the Old Testament and the **coming** of the Word made Flesh, and deepens the **longing** for Jesus to come again.

Teaching and learning process: *learning outcomes*

By the end of this section of work, students should:

- appreciate the importance of hope for human life
- appreciate Advent and Christmas as the Church's celebration of hope and its fulfilment
- appreciate the challenge this hope offers to the world.

Research

Students will have the opportunity to investigate and reflect upon:

- hopes they have for themselves and hopes others have for them
- the qualities hope demands and develops; the challenge of being prepared to wait; the tension between hope and our 'instant' world.

Revelation

Students will have the opportunity to learn about and reflect upon:

- how the Scripture and Tradition of Advent and Christmas form the expectations of Christians
- the hope Advent and Christmas offer the world and how this presents a challenge.

Response

Students will evaluate and reflect upon their learning. They will be given opportunities to make connections between their own experience and Revelation. They will:

- have the opportunity to reflect on their experiences of hope and waiting
- demonstrate knowledge and understanding of the significance of the Church's celebration of Advent and Christmas
- demonstrate appreciation of how the 'O' Antiphons may be used for Advent prayer and reflection
- be able to evaluate the extent to which the hope celebrated in Advent and Christmas challenges the commercialism of this season.

At each stage, select activities to fulfil the learning outcomes.

In Y7 the focus was on Christmas and in Y8 on Advent; here the focus is on the two seasons as celebrations of the hope that finds its fulfilment in Jesus.

Research

- *Looking ahead* (p. 32): focuses on personal level; leads to story of a dream fulfilled, *The Epics*, *Copymaster 9*.
- *Reflect* (p. 32): clarity about word usage prepares for work in *Revelation* on Christian hope.

Revelation

- **Diagnostic assessment,** *Think back* (p. 33), assesses prior learning about Advent (Y8, 1E).
- *Reasons for living and hoping* (pp. 33–4) focuses Advent themes through the 'O' Antiphons; links back to 1C, expectations of the Messiah; explores different ways of naming God; for less able students a simpler text would be 'O come, O come, Emmanuel'. Class project: identifying key themes.
  Reflect (p. 36): Latin: ***E**mmanuel*, ***R**ex*, ***O**riens*, *Clavis*, ***R**adix*, ***A**donai*, ***S**apientia*.
- **Formative assessment 1**, *Classwork* (p. 34)
- *Christmas time* (p. 35): focus on Church's Christmas celebrations; leads to *Think and talk* – reflection and discussion on how the feast impacts or not on neighbourhood, society.
- **Formative assessment 2:** *Homework* (p. 35)
- Extension options: *Copymaster 10,* Advent readings exploring hope.
- **Elsewhere in *Icons***: Unit 2 begins with a study of the gospel proclamation of the transforming mission of Jesus, his power to bring fulfilment and to challenge those he met.

Response *(p. 36)*

- think deeper, apply learning (*Reflect*, write an Advent hymn)
- literacy (*Glossary*)
- ***Summative assessment*** (*Assessment*)
- think wider (*Dilemma*)
- recognise belief (*Living faith*)
- extended discussion/essay writing (*Go further*).

Tips for teachers

Resources

Liturgical Calendar/Spirit of the Season: Liturgy Office website: www.liturgy.demon.co.uk

For teachers:
JD Crichton, *Preparing for Christmas* – the significance of the 'O' Antiphons (Columba Press)

Spiritual and moral links

Living with hope is crucial for human development.

Additional activities

- ◆ The school term finishes before Christmas. Discuss how far the school community celebrations can/should anticipate Christmas.
- ◆ Identify what practical ways the year group/class can help keep the real message of Advent alive in school while not preventing the joyful anticipation of Christmas.
- ◆ Research the hope many groups and organisations offer to the homeless during the Christmas season. Why do they do this?

Doctrinal content

1E: Through the prophets God forms his people in the hope of salvation, in the expectation of a new and everlasting Covenant intended for all, to be written on their hearts. (*CCC* 64) When the Church celebrates the liturgy of Advent each year, she makes present this ancient expectancy of the Messiah, for by sharing in the long preparation for the Saviour's first coming, the faithful renew their ardent desire for his second. (*CCC* 524)

Foundations in Year 8

Students should:

- ◆ appreciate the significance of elements of time – past, present and future – in people's lives
- ◆ understand Advent is the Church's season for celebrating the past, present and future time of Jesus and his mission
- ◆ know and understand the role of prophets in Scripture.

Links to curriculum directory – KS3

The work in this section relates to the following aspects of the *RECD*. They are revisited and deepened throughout *Icons*. The learning outcomes for this section present the *RECD* for classroom use:

- ◆ the concept of Messiah in the Old and New Testament; – Jesus is God become man so that human beings might share the life of God (p. l 7 – Jesus Christ)
- ◆ the development of the Church's faith that Jesus Christ is the Son of God: in the Gospels and New Testament writings; – the Church's faith in Jesus deepens and is handed down through Christian communities (p. 22 – one and holy)
- ◆ the Church's role as witness in society; – in the Church Christ's mission continues; the Church's pastoral role: to be a revelation of God's love and forgiveness, the teacher and servant of the People of God (p. 22 – mission).

For reflection

Question:
How strong is my hope?

If you do not hope, you will not fnd what is beyond your hopes.
(St Clement of Alexandria)

The waiting of the feminine is there and was there always, born with the feminine, always alive in the feminine. It was the waiting of creation itself, the waiting which is at the heart of time where out of a longing the stars are made and the child is formed and born. How could one not have known that all the light and shining things coming out of the darkness of the beginning were made out of this waiting which neither the darkness could quench nor any sun, however great, burn away?
(Laurens van der Post, *About Blady*)

Hope is the glue that holds faith and love together.

Hope has two lovely daughters: courage and anger.
(St Augustine of Hippo)

Catholic teaching

Hope is the theological virtue by which we desire the Kingdom of heaven and eternal life as our happiness, placing our trust in Christ's promises and relying not on our own strength, but on the help of the grace of the Holy Spirit.

The virtue of hope responds to the aspiration to happiness which God has placed in the heart of every person: hope:

- inspires and purifies our activities so as to order them to the Kingdom of heaven
- keeps us from discouragement
- sustains us during times of abandonment
- opens our hearts in expectation of heaven
- preserves us from selfishness
- leads to the happiness that comes from charity.

(*CCC* 1817–8)

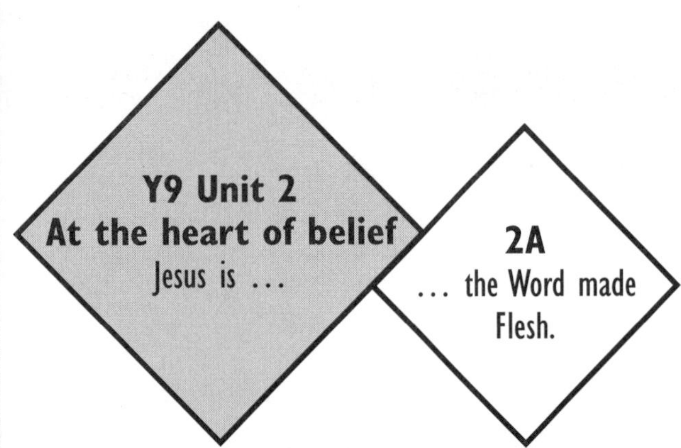

Summary of key learning

Jesus, the **Word made Flesh**, by his words and acts transforms the lives of men and women. In his **Incarnation** the mystery of God's love is revealed.

Teaching and learning process: *learning outcomes*

By the end of this section of work, students should:

- be able to recognise and evaluate when events are 'life-changing'
- know and understand that the gospels proclaim the transforming power of Jesus the Christ
- appreciate something of the mystery of Jesus and the challenge of his question: "Who do you say I am?"

Research

Students will have the opportunity to investigate and reflect upon:

- how a particular moment or time can have far-reaching consequences for the people involved and can be 'life-changing'.

Revelation

Students will have the opportunity to learn about and reflect upon:

- gospel passages which proclaim the transforming power of Jesus
- the ways in which Christian art and Tradition have used gospel sources to reflect on, wonder at and explore the mystery of Jesus
- the challenge of Jesus' question: "Who do you say I am?"; and the Church's belief that every human person must face this question.

Response

Students will evaluate and reflect upon their learning. They will be given opportunities to make connections between their own experience and Revelation. They will:

- have opportunities to reflect upon and appreciate life-changing moments
- show knowledge and appreciation of how the gospels proclaim the transforming power of Jesus
- be able to select and illustrate how Christian art and tradition explore the mystery and majesty of Jesus
- have had the opportunity for personal reflection on Jesus' question: "Who do you say I am?"

At each stage, select activities to fulfil the learning outcomes.

Research

- *Suddenly one day* (pp. 37–8): examples of life-changing events. If you use alternative current situations, ensure that they lead to a positive conclusion.
- *Carpe diem* (p. 38): opportunities for personal reflection and creative use of multi-media; possible link to film *Dead Poet's Society*.

Revelation

- *Jesus makes a difference* (p. 39): link the hymn of praise at the beginning of John's gospel to three individuals for whom an encounter with Jesus leads to transformation. How might each answer the question "Who do you say I am?" These are baptismal stories about new ways of responding, privileged gospels for the three scrutinies of the Rite of Christian Initiation of Adults. The heart of Revelation is God's 'plan of loving goodness'. (*CCC* 51) The stages of revelation (cf *CCC* 54–67) are focused through God's covenant. The key figures of salvation history discover the truth of God's love – 'I Am for You'. Jesus is the fullness of this revelation.
- **Formative assessment 2**, *Homework*: (p.39).
- Who do you say that I am? (p. 39): Peter's response of faith.
- **Diagnostic assessment,** *Think back* (p. 39): assesses learning about Messiah (check answers in 1C, pp. 22, 24).
- *What happened next?* (p. 39): focuses on the role Jesus gave Peter. Extension option: for extended writing or discussion.
- *Jesus, the Saviour for all time* (pp. 40–1): research should raise questions about Christian commitment to Jesus today; and range as widely as time allows, for example, letters to public figures – for example, athletes – who acknowledge their Christian faith. Focus on the Good News of the Saviour through Misereor cloths, a kind of modern 'stained glass'; picture bibles.
  Copymaster 11: Notes for Misereor cloth
- **Formative assessment 1**, *Classwork*: (p. 40).
- **Elsewhere in *Icons***: the transforming power of Jesus and the challenge of his gospel are further focused in 2B in his new commandment; in 2D in the resurrection and in 3B, the transforming power of his Holy Spirit (cf *CCC* 690).

Response *(p. 42)*

- think deeper (*Reflect*)
- literacy (*Glossary*)
- **Summative assessment** (*Assessment*)
- recognise expression of faith (*Living faith*)
- provoke questioning (*Dilemma*)
- opportunity for extended discussion/essay writing (*Go further*)

Tips for teachers

Resources

Seeing Salvation, 90 minute video + 48pp. booklet (BBC Education, Box 20, Tonbridge TN12 6WU)
The Image of Christ in the National Gallery, 12 slides, 12 A3 posters (National Gallery Publications)

For teachers:
Jesus, Self-portrait by God, Enda Lyons (Columba Press, 1994)

Spiritual and moral links

People and situations can transform us when we allow them.

Additional activities

- Link back to the work on saints (Y8, 3D). Look again at some of the saints students studied and discuss how knowing Jesus transformed their lives. In written text, by recording on tape or video create a 'Knowing Jesus' presentation with your chosen saints as narrators.
- Build on work done in Y7, 1B, 'Portraits of Jesus'. Look at images of Jesus in classical and modern art. How does each artist answer Jesus' question "Who do you say I am?". Choose one that expresses your answer or create your own piece of art in a picture, words, music or design.

Doctrinal content

2A: The Word became Flesh *so that we might know God's love*: 'In this the love of God was made manifest among us, that God sent his only Son into the world, so that we might live through him. For God so loved the world that he gave his only Son, that whoever believes in him should not perish but have eternal life.' (*CCC* 458)

Foundations in Year 8

Students should:

- appreciate and recognise evidence of the spiritual and moral nature of the person
- know and understand Christian belief that God calls (vocation) and how people respond (search, faith and commitment)
- know and understand that Luke's gospel presents Jesus, the Universal Saviour.

Links to curriculum directory – KS3

The work in this section relates to the following aspects of the *RECD*. They are revisited and deepened throughout *Icons*. The learning outcomes for this section present the *RECD* for classroom use:

- the concept of Messiah in the Old and New Testament; the life and ministry of Jesus, his teaching, parables and miracles; Jesus is God become man so that human beings might share the life of God (p. 17 – Jesus Christ)
- the mission of Jesus as revealed in the New Testament with particular reference to his priestly, prophetic and kingly roles; – as priest, prophet and king Jesus proclaims the kingdom of God (p. 22 – apostolic)
- the gospel portrayal of the New Covenant in Jesus; of commitment and response (p. 38 – law, grace, sin).

For reflection

Question: What transforms my life?

What Christ accomplished is not above our heads, far off in the skies; it is here on this common earth, in simple human terms, in the sheer flesh and blood of our humanity.
(B McDermott, *Word Become Flesh*)

If you want to get across an Idea, wrap it up in a Person.
(Ralph Bunche)

It is only when one sees Jesus as fully and unequivocally human that his Lordship and divinity appears for the staggering mystery that it is.
(Karl Rahner, *Theological Investigations*)

Catholic teaching

It has pleased God, in his goodness and wisdom, to reveal himself and to make known the secret purpose of his will. This brings it about that through Christ, God's Word made flesh, and in his holy spirit, human beings can draw near to the Father and become sharers in the divine nature. By thus revealing himself God, who is invisible, in his great love speaks to humankind as friends.
(*The Dogmatic Constitution on Revelation*, 2)

We believe and confess that Jesus of Nazareth, born a Jew of a daughter of Israel at Bethlehem at the time of King Herod the Great and the Emperor Caesar Augustus, a carpenter by trade, who died crucified in Jerusalem under the procurator Pontius Pilate during the reign of the Emperor Tiberius, is the eternal Son of God made man. He 'came from God', 'descended from heaven', and 'came in the flesh'. For 'the Word became flesh and dwelt among us, full of grace and truth; we have beheld his glory, glory as of the only Son from the Father … And from his fullness have we all received, grace upon grace.' (*CCC* 423)

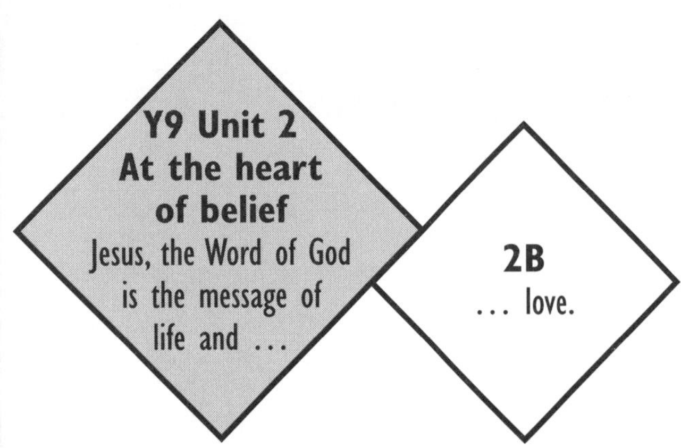

Summary of key learning

Jesus taught that the **greatest commandment** is to **love God** and the second to love one's **neighbour** as oneself for God's sake. His words and deeds challenge and enable people to put this into action.

Teaching and learning process: *learning outcomes*

By the end of this section of work, students should:
- be able to appreciate and evaluate different uses of the word 'love' and the power of love
- know and understand the gospel challenge to 'Love God and one's neighbour as oneself'.

Research
Students will have the opportunity to investigate and reflect upon:
- the different ways in which the word 'love' is used; in conversation, advertising, music, films
- which of these aspects of love are 'passing' and which are 'long-lasting'.

Revelation
Students will have the opportunity to learn about and reflect upon:
- the different ways the gospels record Jesus' dealing with the question: 'Which is the greatest commandment?'; John's washing of feet
- how individual Christians and the Church respond to the challenge in Jesus' response.

Response
Students will evaluate and reflect upon their learning. They will be given opportunities to make connections between their own experience and Revelation. They will:
- be able to present the different ways 'love' is interpreted and expressed today
- demonstrate knowledge and understanding of Jesus' teaching about love of God, self and neighbour
- be able to identify ways in which individual Christians and the Church put Jesus' teaching into action.

At each stage, select activities to fulfil the learning outcomes.

Research
- Starting points (p. 43): current usage of 'love': personal experience, current pop music; explain meaning of chosen texts; analysis exercise: '*How is this love?*'
- *The language of love* (p. 43): introduces definitions proposed by C S Lewis (*The Four Loves*).
- *Evaluate*: personal assessment of learning in this section.
- **Diagnostic assessment:** *Think back* (p. 44) assesses knowledge of and ability to apply Scripture. The quotations do not have to be word accurate.

Revelation
- *This is love* (p. 44): explores the action Jesus names as the sign of his love, the washing of the feet. The Köder picture offers an opportunity for imaginative and personal reflection.
- **Formative assessment 1**, *Classwork*: (p. 44)
- *Love comes first* (p. 45): introduces Jesus' 'new' commandment; focuses understanding through Jesus' parable of the Good Samaritan. NB, Jesus often used parables to shock. How would this shock his listeners? NB, touching the wounded man would have made the priest and Levite unclean. Is this a consideration? (Link to work on groups/politics in Jesus' time, Y8, 1A.)
- *Real love* (pp. 46–7): focuses on Christian response using the prayer of St Francis of Assisi; opportunity for developing the global dimension of Christian love of neighbour. Contacts: CAFOD, Mission Together.
- **Formative assessment 2**, *Homework*: (p. 47)
- **Elsewhere in *Icons*:** Jesus' challenge to Christians to seek the common good is focused in Y9, 3A.

Response *(p. 48)*
- think deeper (*Reflect*)
- question/challenge (*Dilemma*)
- recognise belief in words of prayer (*Living faith*)
- **Summative assessment** (*Assessment*)
- literacy (*Glossary*)
- opportunity for extended discussion/essay writing (*Go further*).

Tips for teachers

Resources

'*The Washing of the Feet*', Sieger Köder, poster size reproduction, St Paul Multi-media Productions)

In Celebration of Love: Paths to Prayer, book and slides, Anne White (St Paul Multi-media Productions, 1997)

CAFOD's *fairground*, magazine for secondary schools

For teachers:

The Four Loves, C S Lewis (Fontana, first published 1960)

Spiritual and moral links

Love is a decision.

Additional activities

- Interview a young engaged or newly married couple and an elderly couple, widow or widower. Ask them what 'love' means to them. What are/were their expectations of married love? What are/were their joys and sorrows? How does love change? Grow?
- Love is … How might the following complete the sentence: a mother, a father, a homeless person, a member of CAFOD, a priest, a missionary. Compare your answers with the definitions of love you have studied.
- Use 1 Corinthians 13, Love is … for reflection. How would this stand as a description of the class, year group, school community?

Doctrinal content

2B: The most fundamental passion is love, aroused by the attraction of the good. (*CCC* 1765) 'To love is to will the good of another'. (*CCC* 1766) Charity is the theological virtue by which we love God above all things for his own sake, and our neighbour as ourselves for the love of God. (*CCC* 1822)

Foundations in Y8

Students should:

- be able to identify unity and division in human life
- know and understand Christian teaching about the role of conscience
- appreciate the challenge to be 'one world'
- appreciate what it means to call the Church 'the People of God'.

Links to curriculum directory – KS3

The work in this section relates to the following aspects of the *RECD*. They are revisited and deepened throughout *Icons*. The learning outcomes for this section present the *RECD* for classroom use:

- the meaning and significance of the commandments that relate to love of God; – the understanding and interpretation of the commandments in the history and tradition of the Church (p. 38 – love of God)
- the meaning and significance of the commandments which relate to love of neighbour and self; Gospel evidence of how the teaching of Jesus reinforced and developed the commandments of the Old Law; – the commandments and teaching of Jesus are a source of inspiration and positive guidance for Christian social and moral life (p. 38 – love of neighbour).

For reflection

Question: How does love energise me?

It is only with the heart that one sees correctly.
What is essential is invisible to the eyes.
(A St Expurey, *The Little Prince*)

Love is relationship. It is a state of being.
Love existed before any human being.
Before we existed, love already existed.
(Anthony de Mello, *Walking on Water*)

Some day, after mastering the winds, the waves, the tides and gravity, we shall harness for God the energy of love, and then, for the second time in the history of the world, man will discover fire.
(Pierre Teilhard de Chardin)

Catholic teaching

Jesus makes charity the *new commandment*. By loving his own 'to the end', he manifests the Father's love which he receives. By loving one another, the disciples imitate the love of Jesus which they themselves receive. Whence Jesus says: "As the Father has loved me, so have I loved you; abide in my love." And again: "This is my commandment, that you love one another as I have loved you." (*CCC* 1823)

The practice of the moral life animated by charity gives to the Christian the spiritual freedom of the children of God … (*CCC* 1828)

The fruits of charity are joy, peace and mercy …
(*CCC* 1829)

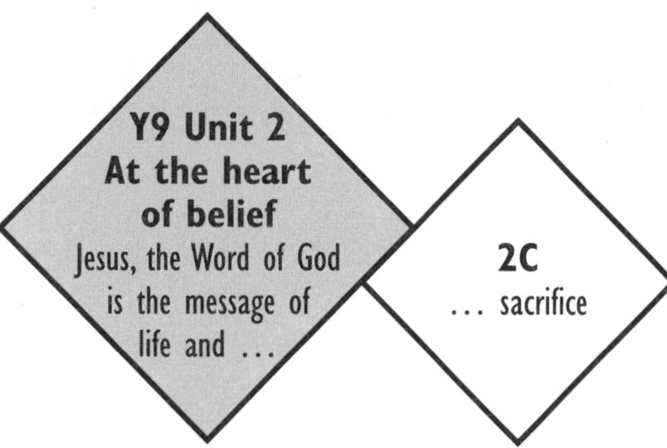

Summary of key learning

In **obedience** to his Father, Jesus accepted his death on the cross. The Sacrament of the Eucharist represents this **sacrifice** and the Church is united with Jesus in his **offering** to the Father.

Teaching and learning process: *learning outcomes*

By the end of this section of work, students should:

- know and appreciate how 'sacrifice' is part and parcel of life
- know and understand the Church's belief that the Sacrament of Eucharist is a living memorial of Jesus' sacrifice.

Research

Students will have the opportunity to investigate and reflect upon:

- how loving can involve 'sacrifice', for example, bringing up a child, caring, education, saying goodbye, work, career.

Revelation

Students will have the opportunity to learn about and reflect upon:

- the Eucharist as the living memorial of Jesus' sacrifice:
  - the Church gathered to remember
  - the proclamation of salvation (Liturgy of the Word)
  - the celebration of communion.

Response

Students will evaluate and reflect upon their learning. They will be given opportunities to make connections between their own experience and Revelation. They will:

- be able to identify 'sacrifice' as part of the human experience of life
- demonstrate knowledge and understanding of the Church's belief that the Eucharist is the living memorial of Jesus' sacrifice
- be able to explain the Church's belief that all are called to share Christ's sacrifice.

At each stage, select activities to fulfil the learning outcomes.

Research

- *The greatest love* (p. 49): there are several versions of this story; the name of the town and the characters change but the message is constant.

Revelation

- *Love and sacrifice* (pp. 50–1): Eucharist as sacrifice for all and assurance of love and forgiveness.
- **Diagnostic assessment:** *Think back* (p. 51) assesses knowledge and understanding of the Mass (Y7, 3D).
- *Do this in memory of me* (p. 50): Eucharist as living memorial approached through development of understanding in early Church – conversations with Simon Peter; and development of personal commitment – Michael's statement. Catholic teaching makes the connection between sacrifice and adoration. Both acknowledge God as above all and worthy of all love and service. (*CCC* 2099) Old and New Testament insist that sacrifice must come from and with the heart. Outward sacrifice must be a sign of spiritual adoration. (*CCC* 2100) Extension option: *An everlasting covenant.*
- *It is right to give God thanks and praise* (pp. 52–3): work with texts from *Eucharistic Prayer for Masses for Various Needs and Occasions* (1995, from the Liturgy Office). Alternatively, use one of the four Eucharistic prayers in a missal.
- *Bread and wine: body and blood* (p. 54): focuses on symbol and mystery through the prayers of offering; link to work on grain of wheat imagery in Y8, 3A.
- **Formative assessment 2**, *Homework*: (p. 54) Extension option: extended writing.
- **Formative assessment 1**, *Classwork: Do this in memory of me* (p. 55): A and B develop work on Eucharist through Years 7 and 8. C offers opportunity to deepen understanding by making connections with Scripture texts.
- **Elsewhere in *Icons***: this work on the sacrifice of Jesus leads into the next section on resurrection, 2D.

Response *(p. 56)*

- literacy (*Glossary*)
- **Summative assessment** (*Assessment*)
- think deeper (*Reflect*)
- challenge thinking (*Dilemma*)
- relate to words of prayer (*Living faith*)
- opportunity for extended discussion/essay writing (*Go further*).

Tips for teachers

Resources

Loaves of Thanksgiving – video (Housetop Publications)

For teachers: *One Bread, One Body* (Catholic Bishops' Conference of England and Wales)

Spiritual and moral links

There is a cost for everything in life, a sacrifice to be made.

Additional activities

- Use Dürer's 'Praying Hands' as an alternative story of sacrifice. Albrecht Dürer and Franz Kingstein were fellow art students. Although they worked as labourers they could not earn enough to support themselves. On the toss of a coin it was decided that Albrecht would carry on studying, Franz would work. When Albrecht began to sell his paintings, he went to Franz with money that would enable him to continue his studies. But the manual labour had left Franz's hands twisted and arthritic. He could not control a brush for the delicate work he had once done. Albrecht was amazed at Franz's lack of bitterness and joy in his friend's success. Watching Franz at prayer one day, he sketched his hands and later created his painting.
- Choose a theme for a class/year Mass. Work with the school chaplain to choose readings, prayers, music. In groups prepare a few words of explanation for each part, helping everyone to focus on the meaning of the actions and words.

Doctrinal content

2C: The Eucharist is a sacrifice because it *re-presents* (makes present) the sacrifice of the cross, because it is its *memorial* and because it *applies* its fruit. (*CCC* 1366) In the Eucharist the sacrifice of Christ becomes also the sacrifice of the members of his Body. The lives of the faithful, their praise, sufferings, prayer and work, are united with those of Christ and with his total offering, and so acquire a new value. (*CCC* 1368)

Foundations in Year 8

Students should:

- appreciate how Christ's sacrifice present on the altar makes it possible for all generations of Christians to be united with his offspring
- know and understand Jesus' invitation to 'fullness of life'
- appreciate the reality of human imperfection and sinfulness and its consequences within the Church
- understand what it means to say that the Church is 'the communion of saints'.

Links to curriculum directory – KS3

The work in this section relates to the following aspects of the *RECD*. They are revisited and deepened throughout *Icons*. The learning outcomes for this section present the *RECD* for classroom use:

- the Church's different ways of naming the Sacrament of the Eucharist and the significance of these names; – participation in the Eucharist and different ministries;– the Eucharist is sacramental sacrifice, thanksgiving, memorial and presence (p. 30 – baptism, confirmation, Eucharist)
- the mission of Jesus as revealed in the New Testament with particular reference to his priestly, prophetic and kingly roles; – as priest, prophet and king Jesus proclaims the kingdom of God (p. 22 – apostolic)
- human response to God's call to a covenant relationship and how this involves blessing, grace, struggle and weakness (original sin); – Scripture and Tradition reveal God's love, mercy and forgiveness which meet human faithfulness and sinfulness (p. 17 – creation).

For reflection

Question: Who gives to me? To whom do I give?

In their wider context [the bread and wine] are symbols of the whole created order which, in Christ, is about to be taken up, refashioned and reborn. The prayers are addressed to 'Lord, God of all creation'. They are prayers of blessing, of thanksgiving for all the blessings which we receive: the gift of life, of goodness, of created beauty, of the satisfaction of purposeful activity, of ingenuity and inventiveness, of the marvels of science and the wonders of outer space. They are prayers and actions by which the whole of that created realm is placed on the altar, and offered to God in whom they have their origin and, indeed, in whom they will find their fulfilment. What is more, these prayers help us to recognise our own role in that great and cosmic endeavour. It is not the raw forces of nature which are there as our offering. Rather it is 'the work of human hands', our best efforts to shape and fashion that reality, to work with it for the common good. It is every venture by which we have tried to develop the created order, harness its potential for good and draw out its beauty.

(Vincent Nichols, *Promise of Future Glory*)

Catholic teaching

The Eucharist is the memorial of Christ's Passover, the making present and the sacramental offering of his unique sacrifice, in the liturgy of the Church which is his Body.

Because it is the memorial of Christ's Passover, the Eucharist is also a sacrifice. The sacrificial character of the Eucharist is manifested in the very words of institution: 'This is my body which is given for you' and 'This cup which is poured out for you is the New Covenant in my blood.' In the Eucharist Christ gives us the very body which he gave up for us on the cross, the very blood which he 'poured out for many for the forgiveness of sins'. (*CCC* 1362, 1365)

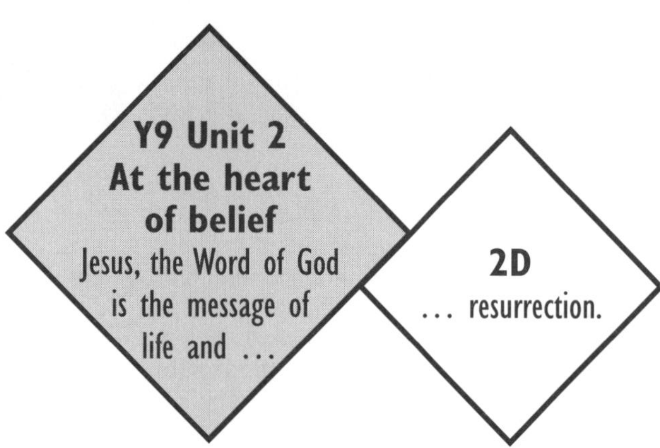

Summary of key learning

The **resurrection** of Jesus is the **heart of Christian faith**. In the light of the resurrection every **human life is precious** and **death is not an end** but a beginning of new life. The **funeral Mass** is an act of faith in the resurrection and in God's promise of **eternal life**.

Teaching and learning process: *learning outcomes*

By the end of this section of work, students should:
- know and appreciate how strong the desire for life is in people
- appreciate why the resurrection of Jesus informs the whole of Christian faith
- know and appreciate Catholic belief and teaching about life after death.

Research

Students will have the opportunity to investigate and reflect upon:
- evidence that the will to live is one of the most powerful of human instincts
- different ways people try to deal with the reality of death: hopes and fears, beliefs about life after death.

Revelation

Students will have the opportunity to learn about and reflect upon:
- how belief in the reality of power of the resurrection is proclaimed in:
  - the gospels and the early Church
  - the life of the Church today (liturgy, daily life, belief in life after death)
- what the Church believes and teaches about life after death.

Response

Students will evaluate and reflect upon their learning. They will be given opportunities to make connections between their own experience and Revelation. They will:
- be able to identify a range of views about life, death and life after death
- demonstrate knowledge and understanding of how belief in the resurrection of Jesus informs all Christian life and faith
- be able to explain Catholic belief in life after death.

At each stage, select activities to fulfil the learning outcomes.

Research

- Photographs (p. 57): focus on human instinct to protect life; leads to *Imagine this*: personal reflection.
- *What price a life?* (p. 57): develops concept of the value of life; invites reflection about risk and death.

Revelation

- *Time of death* (p. 58): explores experiences of and responses to death: sympathy cards; additional texts on *Copymaster 12*: *On death and dying.*
- **Diagnostic assessment:** *Think back* recalls work done in Y7, 2C; Mary Magdalen was the first messenger of the resurrection.
- *Rest in peace* (p. 59): Christian approach to death through a personal statement – Ben's story. Preparation for exploration of Church's prayers.
- **Formative assessment 2**, *Homework: Copymaster 13: Prayers from the Funeral Mass.* Faith does not protect people from the reality of death, calamity and suffering. The promise of eternal life offers hope when life events seem to contradict the good news of the gospel. (cf *CCC* 164)
- *The Resurrection of Jesus* (p. 60): group work with gospel texts. Themes to follow: (a) the disciples' disbelief changes to faith; (b) Jesus is the same and different; (c) Jesus gives the disciples instructions/tasks.
- **Formative assessment 1**, *Classwork*: (p. 60) Extension options (p. 60): drama, multi-media work; *Copymaster 14: I believe! We believe!* Links can be made to a martyr's willingness to risk death and 'welcome' death.
- **Elsewhere in *Icons***: the Church's belief in life after death is confirmed and strengthened by Jesus' promise of the kingdom: this is developed through study of the four last things in 3A and kingdom living in 3D.

Response *(p. 61)*

- **Summative assessment** (*Assessment*)
- reading between the lines, evaluating (*Living faith*)
- challenge thinking (*Dilemma*)
- extended discussion/essay writing (*Go further*)

Tips for teachers

Resources

Your Guide to a Catholic Funeral, (Redemptorist Publications, 1991)

The New Funeral Mass Book, (Redemptorist Publications)

For teachers:
A Grief Observed, C S Lewis (Fontana Books)

Spiritual and moral links

Belief in life after death runs through human history and cultures.

Additional activities

- Research the new rite for a funeral Mass. Look at the readings and prayers of the funeral Mass to see how they:
  - remember that at Baptism the person received life as a member of the Church
  - thank God for the life of the person who has died
  - ask God to grant them mercy, forgiveness and eternal rest
  - recall Jesus' experiences of death and what he taught about life and death
  - encourage people to remember the Church's teaching on life after death and to put their faith in God.

  Try to express this in your own words, or find or draw a symbol to sum up this teaching.
- Discuss how and why at times of major crises/tragedies many people turn to the Church for strength and comfort. What does the Church have to offer those who are bereaved?

Doctrinal content

2D: We firmly believe, and hence we hope that, just as Christ is truly risen from the dead and lives for ever, so after death the righteous will live for ever with the risen Christ and he will raise them up on the last day. Our resurrection, like his own, will be the work of the Most Holy Trinity. (*CCC* 989)

Foundations in Year 8

Students should:

- appreciate the wonder and mystery of being human
- appreciate that reverence for creation is a human instinct
- know and understand how the Church receives God's love, mercy, forgiveness and healing in two sacraments: Reconciliation and Anointing of the Sick
- know and appreciate gospel imagery about the Kingdom of God and its significance.

Links to curriculum directory – KS3

The work in this section relates to the following aspects of the *RECD*. They are revisited and deepened throughout *Icons*. The learning outcomes for this section present the *RECD* for classroom use:

- humanity as created by God; – the Church's teaching about human life, dignity and vocation (p. 17 – creation)
- the life and ministry of Jesus, his teaching, parables and miracles; – that Jesus is God become man so that human beings might share the life of God (p. 17 – Jesus Christ)
- the development of the Church's faith that Jesus Christ is the Son of God: in the Gospels and New Testament writings; – the Church's faith in Jesus deepens and is handed down through Christian communities (p. 22 – one and holy).

For reflection

Question: Who wants to live for ever?

Recognising resurrection

In the midst of a wounded world, you can still hear the heartbeat of God's creation: without a sign of hope today, parents live for tomorrow; residents make plans for their environment when experience says that all their efforts will be fruitless. It is not the powerlessness, but the resilience and power of such people to stay alive in the midst of social neglect that is most striking.

(Austin Smith, *Passion for the Inner City*)

We hardly know in what proportions and under what guise our natural faculties will pass over into the final act of the vision of God. But it can hardly be doubted that, with God's help, it is here below that we give ourselves the eyes and the heart which a final transfiguration will make the organs of a power of adoration, and of a capacity for beatification, particular to each individual man and woman among us.

(Pierre Teilhard de Chardin, *Le Milieu Divin*)

Catholic teaching

The eighth day. For us a new day has dawned: the day of Christ's Resurrection. The seventh day completes the first creation. The eighth day begins the new creation. Thus, the work of creation culminates in the greater work of redemption. The first creation finds its meaning and its summit in the new creation in Christ, the splendour of which surpasses that of the first creation. (*CCC* 349) The Church teaches that every spiritual soul is created immediately by God – it is not 'produced' by the parents – and also that it is immortal: it does not perish when it separates from the body at death, and it will be reunited with the body at the final Resurrection. (*CCC* 366) Although the Resurrection was an historical event that could be verified by the sign of the empty tomb and by the reality of the apostles' encounters with the risen Christ, still it remains at the very heart of the mystery of faith as something that transcends and surpasses history. (*CCC* 647)

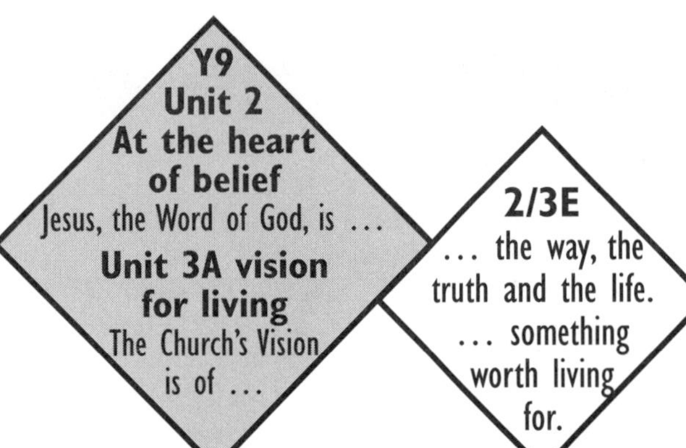

Summary of key learning

Religion influences people in the way they choose to live and the **society** they build. In **Jesus**, Christians see the **way, the truth and the life** to which they are called. Jubilee is a call to **search, witness** and **challenge** contemporary attitudes, beliefs and values.

Teaching and learning process: *learning outcomes*

By the end of this section of work, students should:

- have an appreciation of how religion affects people's lives
- know and understand that Jesus is the Way, the Truth and the Life for the world
- have a critical appreciation of the tension that exists between the gospel message and contemporary cultures.

Research

Students will have the opportunity to investigate and reflect upon:

- evidence of the effects of religion on: individuals, countries, the global community; and benefits and tensions this shows.

Revelation

Students will have the opportunity to learn about and reflect upon:

- how Jesus – the Way, the Truth and the Life – offers something worth living for:
  – The Way: continuing the mission of Jesus; the Truth: proclaiming the good news of Jesus; the Life: living his kingdom values now
- how Christian faith inspires and influences people in their search for personal fulfilment
- some ways in which the gospel vision of personal fulfilment challenges media presentations of success, ambitions, choices and so on.

Response

Students will evaluate and reflect upon their learning. They will be given opportunities to make connections between their own experience and Revelation. They will:

- be able to illustrate and evaluate the influence of religion in the global community
- be able to explain, in broad terms, the Church's belief that Jesus is the Way, the Truth and the Life
- have opportunities to reflect on how this belief affects the search for personal fulfilment
- be able to evaluate the vision of success that the media promotes in the light of the gospel.

At each stage, select activities to fulfil the learning outcomes.

Research

- Religion is … (p. 62): spider graph focus for brainstorm, identifying positive and negative influences on contemporary society; one sentence summary agreed by class.
- Photos (p. 62): contemporary examples may be added from news media.
- **Diagnostic assessment:** *Think back* (p. 62) assesses learning in *Icons* on the gospel proclamation of Jesus. Gospel quotes need not be word accurate.

Revelation

- *A life for the world* (p. 63): focuses on the 'I am' statements in John's gospel; John's message that Jesus is God's answer to human hopes and needs (link back to Y7, 1B, Jesus is God's answer). Leads to reflection on Christian witness and commitment to Christ.
- **Formative assessment 1**, *Classwork*: (p. 63)
- **Formative assessment 2**, *Homework*: (p. 63)
- *The way, the truth and the life* (pp. 64–5): focuses on discipleship that leads to mission to proclaim the good news; introduce Jubilee, time for freedom, worship, renewal: explored through CAFOD Jubilee song – making jubilee real. Post millennium focus could be on why Jesus' birth sets the world's calendar; research into and discussion of millennium celebrations could raise issues of what is valued by the Church, by society. What difference has come from the celebration of Jubilee?
- *Class project: Witnesses in every walk of life* (p. 65): individual projects; focus on people who have found something worth living for. *Copymaster 15, Model for a witness profile,* offers a model for style.
- **Elsewhere in *Icons***: if this section is used in the Spring term it will lead in to work on the common good, Y9, 3A; if it is the final section of work for Y9 it can serve as a summary of the gospel message students have studied throughout *Icons*.

Response *(p. 66)*

- think deeper (*Reflect*)
- literacy (*Glossary*)
- **Summative assessment** (*Assessment*)
- faith in the words of song/prayer (*Living faith*)
- challenge thinking (*Dilemma*)
- extended discussion/essay writing (*Go further*).

Tips for teachers

Resources

Cry Freedom – video (Marble Arch Productions)
The Return of the Saints – video (St Paul Productions)
The Spirit of Assisi – video: stories of extraordinary men and women (Oriente Occidente Productions)

For teachers:
Jesus is Risen, Gerald O'Collins SJ (DLT)

Spiritual and moral links

Everyone has beliefs, values that direct and guide their lives.

Additional activities

◆ Jubilee action calls people to 'do justice', but this does not have to wait until a year of Jubilee. As a class, identify Jubilee actions for justice for Year 9 students: within school and out of school. Work with other Year 9 classes to have a whole year approach to Jubilee action. Publicise your action. As a class, choose a Jubilee 'motto' from the work you have done, that will inspire and remind students of the challenge of the Jubilee.

Doctrinal content

2/3E: The way of Christ 'leads to life'; a contrary way 'leads to destruction'. (*CCC* 1696) The first and last point of reference will always be Jesus Christ himself, who is 'the way, the truth and the life'. It is by looking to him in faith that Christ's faithful can hope that he himself fulfils his promises in them, and that, by loving him with the same love with which he has loved them, they may perform works in keeping with their dignity. (*CCC* 1698)

Foundations in Year 8

Students should:

◆ have reflected upon the kind of world they would like to help create
◆ appreciate that reverence for creation is a human instinct
◆ know and understand that Jesus was born, lived, worked and fulfilled his mission within the Jewish community of his time
◆ know and appreciate gospel imagery about the Kingdom of God and its significance.

Links to curriculum directory – KS3

The work in this section relates to the following aspects of the *RECD*. They are revisited and deepened throughout *Icons*. The learning outcomes for this section present the *RECD* for classroom use:

◆ human response to Cod's call to a covenant relationship ... – Scripture and Tradition reveal God's love, mercy and forgiveness which meet human faithfulness and sinfulness (p. 17 – creation)
◆ the Church's role as witness in society; – in the Church Christ's mission continues; – the Church's pastoral role: to be a revelation of God's love and forgiveness, the teacher and servant of the People of God (p. 22 – mission)
◆ opportunities for the exercise of freedom and responsibility in family life, the local church and society: at local, national and global levels; – the Holy Spirit guides the Church in the way of truth (p. 38 – freedom, responsibility, conscience).

For reflection

Question: When I die, what will people say I lived for?

'Blind man planting sunflowers'
Tucked away, at the back of my memory
you are there: blind man
forever planting sunflowers.
From the TV picture you stepped
through eyes to mind, quietly,
just as, in your stillness,
you had moved along a row
dropping into soil the seeds you could not see.
Through days and years
you have worked steadily:
tilling and tending,
sending down roots into my heart.
Your sunflowers bloom in my dark places.

(Anne White)

We may rightly judge that the future of humanity is in the hands of those who can hand on to posterity grounds for living and for hope.

(Vatican II)

The worship of God is not a rule of safety – it is an adventure of the Spirit, a flight after the unattainable.

(Source unknown)

Catholic teaching

The Word became flesh to be our model of holiness: 'Take my yoke upon you, and learn from me.' 'I am the way, and the truth, and the life; no one comes to the Father, but by me.' On the mountain of the Transfiguration, the Father commands: 'Listen to him!' Jesus is the model for the Beatitudes and the norm of the new law: 'Love one another as I have loved you.' This love implies an effective offering of oneself, after his example. (*CCC* 459)

The social character of human beings indicates that the advancement of the human person and the growth of society are dependent on each other. For the origin, the subject and the purpose of all social institutions is and should be the human person, whose life of its nature absolutely needs to be lived in society. And since social life is not something accidental to us, it is through our dealings with others, mutual duties and exchange with our sisters and brothers, that we grow in all our endowments and can respond to our vocation.
(*The Pastoral Constitution on the Church in the World*, 25)

Other faiths
This is a flexible section. The RE Department will decide each year where it will be included.

Islam
... the beginnings of Islam and the five duties.

Summary of key learning

Muhammad is honoured as the **prophet of Islam**. The **Qur'an** is the holy book. Muslims profess their faith in one God, **Allah**, whose qualities they describe with many names. The **five duties** of Islam are the marks of a believer.

Teaching and learning process: *learning outcomes*

By the end of this section of work, students should:

- have an appreciation of the beginnings of Islam and Muhammad its founder
- know about the five duties (pillars) of Islam.

Research

Students will have the opportunity to investigate and reflect upon:

- some aspects of the history of Islam
- key facts about Muhammad
- Muslim communities in Britain.

Revelation

Students will have the opportunity to learn about and reflect upon:

- the declaration of faith
- how Muslims name Allah
- the five duties of a believer.

Response

Students will evaluate and reflect upon their learning. They will be given opportunities to make connections between their own experience and Revelation. They will:

- demonstrate knowledge and understanding of the origins of Islam and its founder, Muhammad
- know how believers profess their faith in and name Allah
- be able to explain the importance of the five duties for followers of Islam.

At each stage, select activities to fulfil the learning outcomes.

Research

- **Diagnostic assessment**: *Think back* (p. 67) assesses understanding of the importance of learning about other faiths and Catholic teaching about respect for other faiths (Y7, Hinduism, Y8 Judaism).
- Map (p. 67): focuses on the beginnings of Islam, Muhammad, its prophet and the Qur'an. Use an atlas to locate the area in global situation. Research the major Islamic countries today.
- Research the Muslim community in Britain and a mosque.

Revelation

The declaration of Faith (p. 68): the words of the declaration; how Islam names God. The Catechism names Muslims as first among those who 'acknowledge the Creator, profess the faith of Abraham and adore the one, merciful God, mankind's judge on the last day'. (*CCC* 842) NB, some statements in the Qur'an are incompatible with Christian faith. For example, the angel Gabriel's words to Mary are the opposite of the Christian New Testament: 'Allah forbid that Allah should have a son.'

- **Formative assessment 2**, *Homework*: (p. 68)
- *The five duties or pillars of Islam* (p. 69): marks of the believer which faithful Muslims perform; they unite believers all over the world.
- **Formative assessment 1**, *Classwork*: (p. 69)

Response *(p. 70)*

- consider another's belief and reflect on one's own (*Reflect*)
- literacy (*Glossary*)
- Summative assessment (*Assessment*)
- think deeper (*Reflect* and *Final thought*).

Tips for teachers

Resources

Islam for Today, (Religion for Today series, OUP)

For teachers:
Website: http://www.theresit.org.uk
Religions in the UK, a multi-faith directory
Getting to Know People of Other Faiths and leaflets on particular faiths, (Bishops' Conference Committee for Other Faiths) Available from CFOC 6a, Cresswell Park, London SE3 9RD: Contacts: The Multi-Faith Centre, Harborne Hall, Old Church Road, Harborne, Birmingham B17 OBE and The Westminster Interfaith Programme, 110 Thornbury Road, Osterley, Middlesex TW7 4NN
Examining Four Religions, Michael Keene (HarperCollins Educational, 1997)

Spiritual and moral links

Faithfulness to prayer and worship encourages and supports believers.

Additional activities

- The second duty/pillar of Islam, *Salat*, is a call to pray five times a day. Research the prayer sequence of Salat. Describe and explain its stages.
- Salat prescribes certain movements. In your experience, how does movement contribute to prayer?
- Discuss how a school could support Muslim students who want to observe Salat during school hours. Why would this be important?

Islam

The plan of salvation also includes those who acknowledge the Creator, in the first place amongst whom are the Muslims; these profess to hold the faith of Abraham and together with us they adore the one, merciful God, humanity's judge on the last day. (*CCC* 841)

Foundations in Year 8

Students should:

- appreciate the importance of cultural, social and religious background for people's understanding of themselves and others
- know that Jesus calls all people to fullness of life.

Links to curriculum directory – KS3

The work in this section relates to the following aspects of the *RECD*. They are revisited and deepened throughout *Icons*. The learning outcomes for this section present the *RECD* for classroom use:

- the Church's teaching about the need to recognise 'seeds of the Word' in other faith communities (p. 22: mission)
- traditions and way of life of other faith communities … community values (p. 38: the human community).

For reflection

He who knows his own self knows God.
(Muhammad, the prophet)

From the Qur'an:

In the name of God, who is merciful:
all praise be to God,
who is the Lord of everything.
We serve no one but you, our God,
and you are the only one
to whom we turn for help.

If I had two loaves of bread, I would sell one and buy hyacinths, for they would feed my soul.

God changes not what is in a people, until they change what is in themselves.

Not so much as the weight of an ant in earth or heaven escapes from the Lord, neither is aught smaller than that, or greater, but is clearly written in God's book.

In the alternation of night and day and what God has created in the heavens and the earth, surely there are signs for a God-fearing people.

Catholic teaching

Who belongs to the Catholic Church?

The whole human race is called to this catholic unity of the People of God ... and to it, in different ways, belong or are ordered: the Catholic faithful, others who believe in Christ, and finally all humanity, called by God's grace to salvation. (*CCC* 836)

The Church's relationship with the Muslims. The plan of salvation also includes those who acknowledge the Creator, in the first place amongst whom are the Muslims; these profess to hold the faith of Abraham, and together with us they adore the one, merciful God, mankind's judge on the last day. (*CCC* 841)

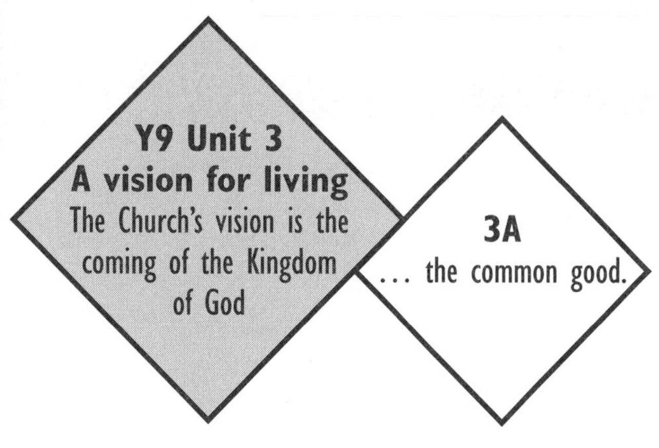

Summary of key learning

Jesus challenges his disciples to work for the **common good** so that all may enjoy **fullness of life**. He uses parables to describe the **judgement** of God on people's choices to **act justly**, accept **social responsibility** and overcome **prejudice** with **respect** for **human dignity**. **Death** puts an end to earthly life and **God's judgement** follows in the light of the choices people have made. **Heaven** and **hell** are not places. Heaven is the joy of life with God. Hell is eternal separation from God.

Teaching and learning process: *learning outcomes*

By the end of this section of work, students should:

- have an appreciation of tensions between 'individualism' and 'the common good'
- know and understand how Jesus challenges Christians to work for the common good.

Research

Students will have the opportunity to investigate and reflect upon:

- opportunities they have to act with others and pursue common aims: at home, in school, in the wider community
- some challenges and tensions that arise between personal good and the common good: who decides.

Revelation

Students will have the opportunity to learn about and reflect upon:

- how Scripture raises questions of social responsibility
- some aspects of the Catholic Church's social teaching in relation to the questions 'Am I my brother's/sister's keeper?'; 'What is the common good?'
- the implications of this teaching for individuals; the local Church; the universal Church; and for life after death.

Response

Students will evaluate and reflect upon their learning. They will be given opportunities to make connections between their own experience and Revelation. They will:

- be able to evaluate some tensions in society between individual rights and responsibilities
- demonstrate knowledge and understanding of Catholic social teaching in terms of the 'common good'
- present evidence of Catholic social teaching in action and evaluate its impact in the life of local and global communities.

At each stage, select activities to fulfil the learning outcomes.

Research

- What makes a team member? (p. 71): focuses on qualities needed for team work through an evaluative exercise.
- Graffiti wall (p. 71): recognise self-interest; role-play develops opposite points of view.
- **Diagnostic assessment,** *Think back*, (p. 71) *:* assesses knowledge and understanding of New Testament images of Church.

Revelation

- *Let justice flow* (p. 72): introduces concept of judgement and justice through parables of sheep and goats (Matthew) and Dives and Lazarus (Luke); links to be made to the work done on conscience in Y8 2D and in Y9 1A. The commandments reveal the nature of God and the human person; they bring religious and social life into unity. One cannot honour others without blessing God: or adore God without loving all his creatures. (*CCC* 2069)
- **Formative assessment 2**, *Homework*: (p. 72)
- *Not the end* (p. 73): brainstorm can serve as diagnostic assessment for what students know or don't know; introduces Church's teaching about the four last things – death (*CCC* 996–7, 1002), judgement (*CCC* 1037–8), heaven (*CCC* 1023–5), hell (*CCC* 1035–6); also purgatory (*CCC* 1031); role-play explores imagery and concepts.
- **Formative assessment 1**, *Classwork*: (p. 74)
- *Love in action* (p. 75): *Class task* – the CAFOD game focuses on action and inaction for justice: *Copymaster 16: On the sidelines.*
- *Who helps?* (p. 75): research into aid and support agencies.
- **Elsewhere in *Icons***: focus on sacraments of service in Y9, 3C is on the lifelong commitment to love and service; and Y9, 3D on living the gospel.

Response *(p. 76)*

- think deeper (*Reflect*)
- challenge thinking (*Dilemma*)
- words for prayer (*Living faith*)
- **Summative assessment** (*Assessment*)
- literacy (*Glossary*)
- apply learning in active response (*Go further*).

Tips for teachers

Resources

The Heart has its Reasons – video (*L'Arche*)
CAFOD – Romero Close, London SW9 9TY
www.cafod.org.uk

For teachers:
The Common Good (Bishops' Conference of England and Wales, 1996)
Belief in Joy, Peter Wilkinson (Mayhew, 1995): the Creed in practical living

Spiritual and moral links

Developing a sense of social responsibility is at the heart of Catholic education.

Additional activities

- Links back or forward to work on Jubilee actions for justice (Y9, 2/3E) and to work on Love (Y9, 2B). Jesus' commandment to love is not separate from the call to justice.
- Take the popular hymn 'Whatsoever you do'. In groups take one verse and illustrate through drama or art the message and the challenge to Christians.
- Plan an education day on global issues with CAFOD advisers.

Doctrinal content

3A: The common good concerns the life of all. (*CCC* 1906) The common good is always oriented towards the progress of persons: 'The order of things must be subordinate to the order of persons, and not the other way around'. This order is founded on truth, built up in justice, and animated by love. (*CCC* 1912)

Foundations in Year 8

Students should:

- have reflected on the kind of world they would like to help create
- be able to identify unity and division in human life
- know and understand the Church's teaching on the origin of sin
- appreciate the reality of human imperfection and sinfulness and its consequences within the Church
- appreciate Christian belief that creation reveals God and human beings are called to be co-creators with God.

Links to curriculum directory – KS3

The work in this section relates to the following aspects of the *RECD*. They are revisited and deepened throughout *Icons*. The learning outcomes for this section present the *RECD* for classroom use:

- images and accounts in Scripture of human success and failure to build and sustain community; Gospel accounts of Jesus' response to issues of justice and relationship; – conflict and its resolution; – Jesus' teaching and example in dealing with some social issues; – the meaning of 'the common good'; (p. 38 – human community)
- the meaning and significance of the commandments which relate to love of neighbour and self; – implications of the commandments for social and moral life – the commandments and teaching of Jesus are a source of inspiration and positive guidance for Christian social and moral life (p. 38 – love of neighbour)
- the Church's vocation to have special care for the poor and oppressed; the Church's role as witness in society; – the Church's pastoral role: to be a revelation of God's love and forgiveness, the teacher and servant of the People of God (p. 22 – mission).

For reflection

Question: In practice how do I answer the question: Who is my neighbour?

Do all the good you can,
In all the ways you can,
In all the places you can,
At all the times you can,
To all the people you can,
As long as ever you can.

(John Wesley)

One of the signs of the present time is the idea of participation, the right that all persons have to participate in the construction of their own common good.

(Oscar Romero)

Communion is not something you do by yourself. For there to be communion, one body has to take hold of another body's hand, and that doesn't happen by accident.

(Source unknown)

Catholic teaching

In keeping with the social nature of man, the good of each individual is necessarily related to the common good, which in turn can be defined only in reference to the human person: do not live entirely isolated, having retreated into yourselves, as if you were already justified, but gather instead to seek the common good together.

By common good is to be understood 'the sum total of social conditions which allow people, either as groups or as individuals, to reach their fulfilment more fully and more easily'. The common good concerns the life of all. It calls for prudence from each, and even more from those who exercise the office of authority. It consists of three essential elements:

- respect for the person as such
- the social well-being and development of the group itself;
- peace, that is, the stability and security of a just order.

(*CCC* 1905–12)

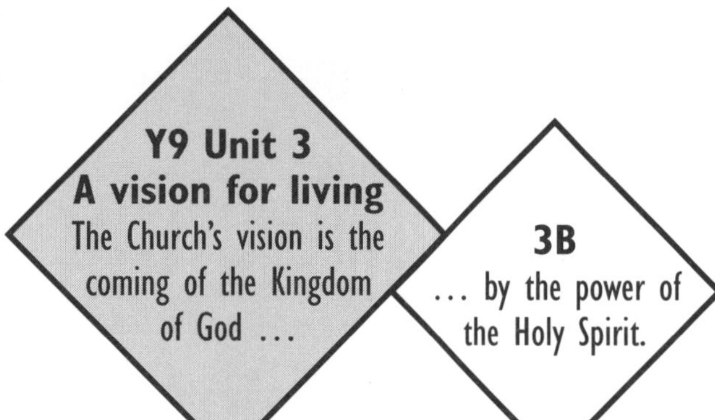

Summary of key learning

By the **power** of the **Holy Spirit**, the **bishops**, under the guidance of the Pope, teach and lead the Church. Their **authority** is a gift that brings responsibility to help people to grow and to respond to the Holy Spirit.

Teaching and learning process: *learning outcomes*

By the end of this section of work, students should:

- be able to evaluate different attitudes to power, privilege and responsibility
- know and understand the Church's teaching about the power of the Holy Spirit and authority in the Church.

Research

Students will have the opportunity to learn about and reflect upon:

- powerful people and where their power comes from in school
- personal experiences of having power and exercising authority; questions this raises, responsibilities, challenges.

Revelation

Students will have the opportunity to learn about and reflect upon:

- how the power of Pentecost is at work in the Church in terms of:
  - the transformation the spirit brings
  - evidence of power
  - exercise of authority
  - organisation and leadership
- structures of responsibility and authority in the local and universal Church: (bishops, Pope, Council, Synod).

Response

Students will evaluate and reflect upon their learning. They will be given opportunities to make connections between their own experience and Revelation. They will:

- be able to illustrate the exercise of power and the challenges it brings
- be able to explain the role of the Holy Spirit in the Church
- demonstrate knowledge and understanding of the Church's teaching about power, responsibility, authority and leadership.

At each stage, select activities to fulfil the learning outcomes.

Research

- *School power* (p. 77): focus on creating a profile of power, authority and responsibility in the school community.
- *Power talk* (p. 77): the power of advertising; the advertising agenda.
- *Power first* (p. 78): some dilemmas that come with power. Possible extension into neighbourhood/national power issues of current interest.

Revelation

- **Diagnostic assessment:** *Think back* (p. 79) assesses knowledge and understanding of the Pentecost event.
- *The gift of power* (p. 79): raises understanding of structures of Church and power in the Church; makes link between the gift of the Holy Spirit and the concept of authority as responsibility for growth and response to the Holy Spirit.
- *The gift of authority* (p. 80): develops understanding of the role of the Holy Spirit in guiding the *Magisterium*; the teaching authority entrusted by Christ to the apostles and their successors – apostolic succession: (*CCC* 880, 896); focuses on authority as service through study of the prayers of ordination of a bishop.
- **Formative assessment 1**, *Classwork*: (p. 80)
- *Pentecost every day* (p. 81): focuses on the power of the Spirit at work in the diversity of gifts in the Church; research into some diocesan and parish organisations.
- **Formative assessment 2**, *Homework*: (p. 81)
- **Elsewhere in *Icons***: further work on charisms (gifts of the Spirit) follows in Y9, 3D.

Response *(p. 82)*

- apply learning (*Reflect*)
- literacy (*Glossary*)
- **Summative assessment** (*Assessment*)
- think deeper (*Reflect*)
- challenge thinking (*Dilemma*)
- faith in words of hymn (*Living faith*)
- opportunity for extended discussion/essay writing (*Go further*).

Tips for teachers

Resources

The History of the Popes – video, Vols 1,2 3 (Acorn Video)

For teachers:
The Spirit of the Father and of the Son, F X Durrell (St Paul's Publications, 1989)

Spiritual and moral links

Everyone has power of some sort. It is how is it used that matters.

Additional activities

- Research ways in which the gifts of the Spirit to the Church are used and developed in parish groups and organisations, the schools of the diocese, support groups in the diocese. Use as source your diocesan year book and/or the Catholic directory. Collate with all the individual work done in FA2. Display it. Choose a suitable heading.
- Find out the motto of your diocese/diocesan bishop and what it means. What links can you make between it and the school motto or mission statement?
- Research the names and mottos of the other 22 dioceses of England and Wales.

Doctrinal content

3B: Christ is himself the source of the ministry in the Church. (*CCC* 874). He instituted the Church. He gave her authority and mission, orientation and goal. 'The bishops, as vicars and legates of Christ, govern the particular Churches assigned to them by their counsels, exhortations and example, but over and above that also by the authority and sacred power which indeed they ought to exercise so as to edify, in the spirit of service which is that of their Master' (*CCC* 894). The duty of Christians to take part in the life of the Church impels them to act as witnesses of the Gospel and of the obligations that flow from it. This witness is a transmission of the faith in words and deeds. (*CCC* 2472)

Foundations in Y8

Students should:
- understand the importance of a sense of vocation for human life
- know and understand how the sacrament of confirmation deepens Christian initiation and vocation
- know and understand Christian teaching about the role of conscience
- have reflected on the kind of world they would like to help to create
- appreciate Catholic teaching about inter-Church relationships.

Links to curriculum directory – KS3

The work in this section relates to the following aspects of the *RECD*. They are revisited and deepened throughout *Icons*. The learning outcomes for this section present the *RECD* for classroom use:
- the role of the Holy Spirit in Old and New Testament; – the Holy Spirit guides and leads the People of God into the truth of the Gospel (p. 17 the Holy Spirit)
- leadership and authority in Scripture and Tradition and in the life of the Church today; – the Church's understanding of leadership, authority and service; the role and apostolic succession of Pope and Bishops (p. 22 – apostolic)
- opportunities for the exercise of freedom and responsibility in family life, the local Church and society: at local, national and global levels; the role of authority in community life: in the family, the Church and society; – of concepts of authority; – the Holy Spirit guides the Church in the way of truth (p. 38 – freedom, responsibility, conscience).

For reflection

Question: By what measure do I use and recognise authority?

For the fulfilment of his purpose God needs more priests, bishops, pastors and missionaries. He needs mechanics and chemists, gardeners and street sweepers, dress designers and cooks, doctors, teachers, shopkeepers and athletes.

(Paul Tournier, quoted in parish newsletter)

No one securely commands but one who has learned to obey.

(Thomas à Kempis)

I slept and I dreamed that life was all joy.
I woke and I found that life was all service.
I served and I found that service was joy.

(Source unknown)

The gospel of the Holy Spirit is written in the lives of Christian men and women.

Catholic teaching

Christ himself is the source of ministry in the Church. He instituted the Church. He gave her authority and mission, orientation and goal. (*CCC* 874)

The ministry in which Christ's emissaries do and give by God's grace what they cannot do and give by their own powers, is called a sacrament by the Church's tradition. Indeed, the ministry of the Church is conferred by a special sacrament. Intrinsically linked to the sacramental nature of ecclesial ministry is its character as service. Entirely dependent on Christ who gives mission and authority, ministers are truly 'slaves of Christ', in the image of him who freely took 'the form of a slave' for us. Because the word and grace of which they are ministers are not their own, but are given to them by Christ for the sake of others, they must freely become the slaves of all. (*CCC* 875–6)

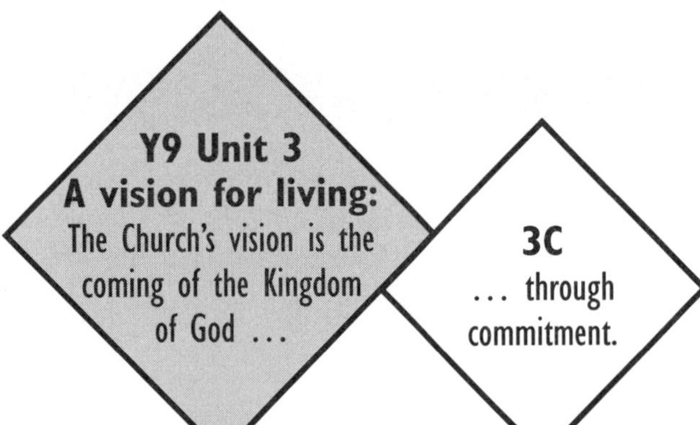

Summary of key learning

Marriage and **Holy Orders** are sacraments at the service of communion. The **commitment** of the priest to Christ and his Church, and of the wife and husband to one another, are a **living witness** of the **loving communion** of the Father, Son and Holy Spirit.

Teaching and learning process: *learning outcomes*

By the end of this section of work, students should:

- be able to evaluate what commitment means and different attitudes to it in the world today
- know and understand the Catholic celebration of the Sacraments of Marriage and Holy Orders.

Research

Students will have the opportunity to investigate and reflect upon:

- how people take on and live commitment, for example, relationships, careers, lifestyle
- different forms of commitment in terms of time, collaboration, degree.

Revelation

Students will have the opportunity to learn about and reflect upon:

- 'communion' and 'commitment' are the gifts of the Sacraments of Marriage and Holy Orders.

Response

Students will evaluate and reflect upon their learning. They will be given opportunities to make connections between their own experience and Revelation. They will:

- show understanding and appreciation of a variety of forms and of attitudes to commitment in society today
- be able to identify in the life of the Church some of the different ways in which people live commitment and communion
- be able to explain how commitment and communion are signs of the Church's faith in God Three in One
- demonstrate knowledge and understanding of how communion and commitment are expressed in the rites and symbols of the Sacraments of Marriage and Holy Orders.

At each stage, select activities to fulfil the learning outcomes.

Research

- Poem (p. 83): focuses on qualities and characteristics of commitment; leads to
- *Words we use* and *Short term, long term* (p. 83), which develop understanding and raise issues and attitudes to commitment.

Revelation

- **Diagnostic assessment:** *Think back* (p. 84): assesses learning about sacraments through *Icons* – Church's naming of sacraments of initiation and healing.
- Celebrating commitment (pp. 84–7): introduces Church's two sacraments of service – signs of the communion of love that is the Church's vocation. (*CCC* 959)
- Marriage: photographs distinguish wedding day/marriage; focus on the prayers and actions of the rite using Copymaster 17. A video or collection of photographs would be the ideal starting point for the study of both sacraments: NB, 'a sacramental celebration is a meeting of God's children with their Father, in Christ and the Holy Spirit; this meeting takes the form of a dialogue, through actions and words.' (*CCC* 1153)
- **Formative assessment 1,** *Classwork*: (p. 85)
- Holy Orders (pp. 86–7): photographs of ordination service; actions and prayers of the rite using *Copymaster 18.*
- **Formative assessment 2,** *Homework*: (p. 87)
- *Questioning commitment* (p. 87): current issues and ideas; how have these been changed/challenged by the learning.
- **Elsewhere in *Icons***: In Y9, 3D, students will study the Christian vision of the kingdom 'on earth and in heaven'.

Response *(p. 88)*

- literacy (*Glossary*)
- **Summative assessment** (*Assessment*)
- think deeper (*Reflect*)
- challenge thinking (*Dilemma*)
- apply learning (*Living faith*).

Tips for teachers

Resources

Your Wedding and *Getting Married* – booklets (Redemptorist Publications)

For teachers:
What binds Marriage? Timothy J Buckley, Roman Catholic Theology in practice (Redemptorist Publications, 1997)

Spiritual and moral links

There is in everyone a need and desire for permanence in relationships.

Additional activities

- Make links with present work (p. 88) with Y9, 3B and the gifts of the Spirit used by the whole community for service in the parish and diocese.
- Research/discuss what current TV soaps present in their portrayals of marriage and priesthood. How do these conflict with, challenge and reflect Church teaching about marriage and priesthood?
- Link back to Y9, 2B and 2C on Love and Sacrifice. In what ways are these elements of marriage and the priesthood?

Doctrinal content

3C: Holy Orders and Matrimony are directed towards the salvation of others. (*CCC* 1534) Through these sacraments those already *consecrated* by Baptism and Confirmation for the common priesthood of all the faithful can receive particular consecrations. Those who receive the sacrament of Holy Orders are *consecrated* in Christ's name to feed the Church by the word and grace of God. On their part, 'Christian spouses are fortified and, as it were, *consecrated* for the duties and dignity of their state by a special sacrament'. (*CCC* 1535)

Foundations in year 8

Students should:

- appreciate how many gifts contribute to the life of a community
- understand what it means to say the Church is 'the communion of saints'
- know and understand Christian belief that God calls (vocation) and how people respond (search, faith, commitment)
- know and understand the significance of anointing as a symbolic act that acknowledges and consecrates vocation.

Links to curriculum directory – KS3

The work in this section relates to the following aspects of the *RECD*. They are revisited and deepened throughout *Icons*. The learning outcomes for this section present the *RECD* for classroom use:

- the rites of the Sacrament of Matrimony and their significance; the joys and demands of married life; – the values and expressions of love and commitment in marriage (p. 30 – matrimony and holy orders)
- the service and sign given by the order of deacons in the Church; the rites of the Sacrament of Holy Orders; – the joys and demands of priesthood (ibid)
- marriage and holy orders are a vocation to service; the strength and blessings of these sacraments for particular ways of life (ibid)
- the Church's understanding of vocation; – the need for a personal response to God (p. 22 – one and holy).

For reflection

Question: What does commitment add to my life?

What is the difference between involvement and commitment? It's like bacon and eggs: the hen is involved, but the pig is committed.

(Anon)

A successful marriage starts today, every day.

(Anon)

The priest is a sign of unity, a symbol of the communion of the people in whose presence and upon whose acclamation he was ordained. The ministerial priesthood serves the common priesthood of all believers. He is a sign of Christ and a sign of the Church, someone who cannot be defined simply in terms of what he does.

True Christian marriage is not just a matter of exchanging rights and duties. It is a sacrament whereby the couple reflect the love of Christ for the Church, they make it visible in their own lives, and in this way they form the 'domestic Church', the most basic of all Christian communities.

(Liam Kelly, *Sacraments Revisited*)

Catholic teaching

Let married people themselves, who are created in the image of the living God and constituted in an authentic personal dignity, be united together in equal affection, agreement of mind and mutual holiness. Thus, in the footsteps of Christ, the principle of life, they will bear witness by their faithful love in the joys and sacrifices of their calling to that mystery of love which the Lord revealed to the world by his death and resurrection.
(*The Pastoral Constitution on the Church in the World Today*, 52)

The purpose for which priests are consecrated by God through the ministry of the bishop is that they should be made sharers in a special way in Christ's priesthood and, by carrying out sacred functions, act as minister of him who through his Spirit continually exercises his priestly role for our benefit in the liturgy.
(*Decree on the Ministry and Life of Priests*, 5)

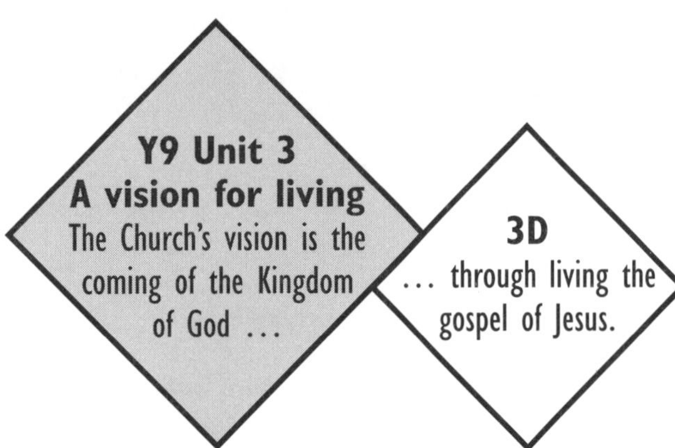

Summary of key learning

The **Church** is called to **evangelise** – to proclaim the Gospel in word and action and so become a **sign of the Kingdom**, the rule of God's love and the communion of the whole human family with the **Trinity**. The **Beatitudes** are the heart of Jesus' teaching. They sum up the **Christian vocation** and proclaim the joy of the Kingdom.

Teaching and learning process: *learning outcomes*

By the end of this section of work, students should:

- appreciate that everyone needs a vision
- know and understand the Christian vision in terms of the Kingdom of God
- be able to evaluate the challenge and influence of this Christian vision in the world today.

Research

Students will have the opportunity to investigate and reflect upon:

- vision statements of some organisations and how these influence them
- personal visions and their impact in daily life; does everyone have a vision for living?

Revelation

Students will have the opportunity to learn about and reflect upon:

- the meaning of 'the Kingdom of God' in Scripture and Tradition
- the Christian vision for today in terms of the Kingdom of God; kingdom people, kingdom action, kingdom challenge
- the influence and challenge of these kingdom values, attitudes and action in our multi-faith, multi-cultural society.

Response

Students will evaluate and reflect upon their learning. They will be given opportunities to make connections between their own experience and Revelation. They will:

- be able to explain, illustrate and evaluate the importance of a vision for everyone
- demonstrate knowledge and understanding of the Church's belief in the Kingdom of God
- be able to select and illustrate appropriate examples of kingdom people, values, actions and challenges
- be able to evaluate evidence of the presence and impact of the Kingdom of God in our world.

At each stage, select activities to fulfil the learning outcomes.

Research

- What is a *vision statement?* (p. 89): research vision statements of local organisations.
- **Diagnostic assessment:** *Test your memory* (p. 89) assesses prior learning and understanding. NB, need to identify class understanding of 'vision' and 'mission' (link back to work in Y7, 1B).
- *Reflect* (p. 89): CAFOD's vision statement.

Revelation

- *One Gospel: Many lives* (p. 90): introduces concept of 'charisms', gifts of the Spirit directed to specific task and evident in response of founders and religious communities; use founders of local religious orders or ones associated with the school if appropriate.
- **Formative assessment 2**, *Homework*: (p. 90) individual mini projects.
- *Jesus' Vision: The Kingdom of God* (pp. 91–3): focuses on Matthew's collection of the beatitudes as a 'vision statement'; and a way into the kingdom (link back to Y9, 3A, *Heaven is not a place*); uses scripture to identify kingdom people, kingdom values in:
- **Formative assessment 1**, *Classwork*: (p. 92)
- *Reflect*: *Kingdom vision* (p. 93); link back to 2/3E if this has been used, or to work in Y8, 3C on gospel imagery.
- *Class projects* (pp. 94–5): groups choose A or B or both as extension work.
  A: focuses on Mary as model disciple and the Magnificat as the song of praise and vision of the kingdom the Church has made its own. (Link back to work on this text in Y7, 2A.)
  B: focuses on Rublev icon of the Trinity as vision of the kingdom – the communion of the Trinity.
  In sharing their work students can be encouraged to see similarities, for example, food and feasting.

Response *(p. 96)*

- literacy (*Glossary*)
- **Summative assessment** (*Assessment*)
- think deeper (*Reflect*)
- challenge thinking (*Dilemma*)
- apply learning (*Living faith*)
- for extended discussion/essay writing (*Go further*)
- creative expression of learning (*Be creative*).

Tips for teachers

Resources

A Passion for Life, Fragments of the Face of God, Joan Chittister
Icons by Robert Lentz, (Orbis Books, 1996): Gospel values in the lives of Christians and non-Christians

For teachers:
Passion for the Possible, Daniel O'Leary (Columba Press, 1998)

Spiritual and moral links

The search for personal happiness is inspired by each one's vision of life.

Additional activities

- Link to work in Y8, 3C on the imagery of the kingdom Jesus uses in his parables of the kingdom. Draw together this section's work under headings: Kingdom People, Kingdom Values, Kingdom Vision, Kingdom Challenge. Students are invited to write/display names, ideas, sentences from their work under these headings.

Doctrinal Content

3D: The Beatitudes teach us the final end to which God calls us: the Kingdom, the vision of God, participation in the divine nature, eternal life, filiation, rest in God. (*CCC* 1726) In the Beatitudes, the New Law fulfils the divine promises by elevating and orienting them toward the 'kingdom of heaven'. It is addressed to those open to accepting this new hope with faith – the poor, the humble, the afflicted, the pure of heart, those persecuted on account of Christ – and so marks out the surprising ways of the Kingdom. (*CCC* 1967)

Foundations in Year 8

Students should:

- understand the significance of being known by name
- appreciate Christian belief that creation reveals God and human beings are called to be co-creators
- know and appreciate gospel imagery about the Kingdom of God and appreciate its significance
- have an appreciation of the challenge to be one world.

Links to curriculum directory – KS3

The work in this section relates to the following aspects of the *RECD*. They are revisited and deepened throughout *Icons*. The learning outcomes for this section present the *RECD* for classroom use:

- Jesus' imagery of 'the kingdom of God'; – the Church's understanding of its nature and role in the world (p. 22 – church)
- the mission of Jesus as revealed in the New Testament with particular reference to his priestly, prophetic and kingly roles; – as priest, prophet and king Jesus proclaims the kingdom of God (p. 22 – apostolic)
- the Church's vocation to have special care for the poor and oppressed; in the Church Christ's mission continues (p. 22 – mission)
- the implications of the commandments for social and moral life; – the commandments and teaching of Jesus are a source of inspiration and positive guidance for Christian social and moral life (p. 38 – love of God and love of neighbour).

For reflection

Question: What is my vision of the kingdom?

Happiness is always a consequence. If you can be grateful you will find the secret of happiness.

(Anthony de Mello, *Walking on Water*)

You are writing a gospel,
a chapter each day,
by the deeds that you do
and the words that you say.
People read what you write,
be it false or true.
Now what is the gospel
according to you?

(Source unknown)

Find the door of your heart and you will find the door of the kingdom of God.

(St John Chrysostom)

Catholic teaching

At the end of time, the Kingdom of God will come in its fullness. After the universal judgement, the righteous will reign for ever with Christ, glorified in body and soul. The universe itself will be renewed. In this new universe, the heavenly Jerusalem, God will have his dwelling among men. He will wipe away every tear from their eyes, and death shall be no more, neither shall there be mourning nor crying nor pain any more, for the former things have passed away.

Far from diminishing our concern to develop this earth, the expectancy of a new earth should spur us on, for it is here that the body of a new human family grows, foreshadowing in some way the age which is to come. That is why, although we must be careful to distinguish earthly progress clearly from the increase of the kingdom of Christ, such progress is of vital concern to the kingdom of God, insofar as it can contribute to the better ordering of human society. (*CCC* 1042–1050)

By living with the mind of Christ, Christians hasten the coming of the Reign of God, 'a kingdom of justice, love and peace'. They do not, for all that, abandon their earthly tasks; faithful to their master, they fulfil them with uprightness, patience and love. (*CCC* 2046)

COPYMASTER 1 Commandments

Jesus' two commandments guide Christians.

Group work

1. Decide which of these attitudes are a response to Jesus' commandments. Mark them 'first', 'second', 'both' or 'no'.

   Positive response to life. ____________________

   Respect for life as God's gift. ____________________

   Negative attitude to life. ____________________

   Lack of respect for God's commandments. ____________________

   Taking responsibility for life. ____________________

   Acting irresponsibly towards life. ____________________

2. Using the attitudes from 1 as headings, group the following actions and attitudes. Are there any that could go under more than one heading?

making peace	cheating	feeding the hungry	envy
helping the poor	loyalty	murder	drugs
pornography	bad example	being greedy	patience
fortune telling	trust in God	standing up for justice	war
prayer	Sunday worship	care for the sick	anger
respect	bullying	child abuse	despair
almsgiving	swearing	jealousy	racism
stealing	revenge	forgiving	
friendship	lies	love and obedience to parents	
helping with younger brothers and sisters	voluntary service overseas		

3. Is there anything you think it would be important to add to this list?

4. Prepare points for a class debate on the following topic:

   'The Commandments: a Guide for Today'.

   Present the case 'for' and 'against'.

The Protestant Reformation

Arguments for reform were debated in Europe and in Britain. The teaching authority of the Church was challenged. Since the Bible was the inspired Word of God, it was sufficient. People should be able to read the Bible in their own language and there was no need for Tradition with the Church as teacher and interpreter. Linked to this was an attack on the number and purpose of the sacraments. Doctrinal arguments centred on 'justification' – grace was a free gift of God, therefore people were saved by faith alone. The attack on the sacraments was also an attack on the Church's administration of the sacraments. It was against these ideas that Henry VIII published his *Defence of the Seven Sacraments against Martin Luther* (1521). He was rewarded by the Pope with the title 'Defender of the Faith'.

In England

Twelve years later the English Church was in schism. **Henry VIII**'s appeal to the Pope to annul his marriage to Queen Catherine had been denied.

In 1533 Parliament passed the Act of Restraint of Appeals affirming the King's juridical power in England. **Thomas Cranmer**, whose appointment as Archbishop of Canterbury had been confirmed by the Pope, declared Henry's marriage to Catherine null and void. Henry married **Anne Boleyn**. The Pope issued a deferred sentence of excommunication against Henry. (Confirmed in 1538.)

In 1534 Henry was declared Supreme Head of the Church in England. The Act of Succession required loyal subjects to take an oath of loyalty to Henry's heirs. This meant acknowledging the divorce and the King's authority in the Church in England. **John Fisher**, Bishop of Rochester, was executed for refusing the oath in 1534. Two weeks later, on 6 July 1534, **Thomas More**, once Henry's Chancellor, was beheaded for the same reason.

In 1536 the dissolution of monasteries began. Lands and goods were confiscated. The king kept the wealth and sold the land to courtiers. (From the shrine of Thomas a Becket: 4,994 ounces of gold, 4,425 of silver gilt, 5,286 of silver and 26 cartloads of other treasure.)

John Houghton, Richard Reynolds and John Stone, all monks, were the first **Tyburn martyrs**. They were executed for their faith on 4 May 1535.

Henry's son, **Edward Vl**, was committed to the Protestant cause. He approved the publication of the *Book of Common Prayer*, laying down the form of services for the Church in England and the doctrines of the Church in 39 articles.

Mary Tudor, daughter of Queen Catherine, was a Catholic. In her persecution of Protestants, Thomas Cranmer was burned as a heretic.

Elizabeth I succeeded Mary. In 1559 the Protestant religion was established by law. Attendance at a Protestant church on Sunday was made obligatory. Those who disobeyed could be fined, though some of the land-owning families were excused and continued as Catholics, paying for this privilege. The Catholic Church in England and Wales was sustained by the faith of men and women who were prepared to die for their faith. Colleges in Douai, Rome and Valladolid provided training for priests.

The Catholic Reformation

The need for change had been recognised in the Church of the later middle ages. After the scandals of the succession of anti-popes, the work of the Council of Constance (1414–1418) reunited the Church. The restoration of the Papacy to Rome brought administrative benefits, but its greater importance was the reassertion of the Pope's authority as the successor of St Peter. The building of the basilica of St Peter's in Rome on the historical site of his tomb was symbolic of this. In the next hundred years successive Councils debated issues such as the pastoral role of bishops, the danger of absentee bishops and their involvement in political affairs at the expense of their pastoral and teaching responsibilities. Pope Eugenius IV promoted holiness of life by example and encouraged reform of religious orders and training of priests. Pope Paul III's work for the **Council of Trent** began in 1534. This came to be the great Council of the Catholic Reformation. It opened in 1545 and lasted over two decades, closing in December 1563.

Teacher's history notes 2

England

Seventeenth and eighteenth centuries

James I of England (James VI of Scotland) was a Scottish Protestant. His name lives on in the *King James Bible*. It was published in 1611 and became the authorised version for the Church of England.

The discovery of the **Gunpowder Plot** (1605) led to a fresh outbreak of persecution of Catholics. Some of the last English and Welsh martyrs died at this time.

Within the Church of England, time brought tensions and changes that led to the formation of groups of **Dissenters**. These groups disagreed with some aspect of the Church of England's life or teaching. For example, the **Puritans** wanted simplicity in worship and banned all statues, candles, rituals and even Christmas celebrations. The hopes and aspirations of the Dissenters led to the formation of a number of religious movements within the Church of England. **John** and **Charles Wesley** led the revival that became the **Methodist Church**. **George Fox** and his followers formed the Society of Friends, the **Quakers**. The **Baptists** only admitted to baptism people who could affirm for themselves their decision to follow Christ. Today this usually means not younger than teenagers.

Some Anglicans looked back to the early days of the Church and became the High Church movement. Each group suffered intolerance at the hands of others.

The climate of suspicion and fear was heightened by the execution of **King Charles I** and the English Civil War. **Charles II** was a Catholic in secret. **James II** was openly Catholic, but his attempts to have Catholicism accepted failed.

In 1688 Parliament invited the Protestant Prince **William of Hanover** and his wife **Mary**, (daughter of James II) to become king and queen of England. In 1701 the Act of Settlement made it unlawful for the king or queen of England, and those in line of succession to be a Catholic or marry a Catholic. This law remains on the statute book.

It was 80 years before an Act of Parliament relaxed the laws against Protestant Dissenters. Even then, Catholics and Jews were still barred from public office, the professions and the universities.

Nineteenth and twentieth centuries

A move towards tolerance began and grew. In 1829 the law of **Catholic Emancipation** meant that Catholics could enter the professions as lawyers, doctors and teachers.

The **Oxford Movement** was a group of Oxford clerics who wanted to stress the Tradition of the Church as well as the Bible. They argued that the apostolic succession (handing on of the authority Jesus gave the apostles) was a guarantee for the authority of the Church. A crucial event for this movement is recognised in a sermon by **John Henry Newman** at Keble College in 1833. Both Newman and **Henry Manning** were received into full communion with the Roman Catholic Church, and later both were named Cardinals. They played key roles in the revival of the Catholic Church in England: Newman at the Oratory in Birmingham and Manning as the second Archbishop of Westminster.

1850 saw the Restoration of the Catholic Hierarchy of England and Wales. **Cardinal Nicholas Wiseman** was the first Archbishop of Westminster. Dioceses were re-established in England and Wales, but articles and cartoons in national newspapers showed that anti-Catholic feeling had not died. Cardinal Manning did a great deal to integrate the Catholics of the old English families, the many Irish immigrants and the converts from other groups. He showed that Catholics could play a part in national life. He was known as a friend of the poor and was accepted as a mediator in the London dock strike of 1889. When he died, the poor lined the streets for his funeral service.

COPYMASTER 4 Some of the Forty Martyrs of England and Wales

The first martyrs were three Carthusian priors executed at Tyburn on 4 May 1535.

Religious orders

- John Houghton, Carthusian, Prior of the London Charterhouse, first of the martyrs under Henry VIII, died aged 45 at Tyburn on 4 May 1535.
- Richard Reynolds, Bridgetine, Syon Abbey, Isleworth, died aged 43 at Tyburn on 4 May 1535.
- John Stone, Austin Friar, died at Canterbury on 27 December 1535.
- Edmund Campion, Jesuit, died at Tyburn on 1 December 1581.
- Nicholas Owen, Jesuit lay brother, died under torture in the Tower of London on 2 March 1606.
- Alban Roe, Benedictine, died at Tyburn on 21 January 1642.
- John Wall, Franciscan, died at Worcester on 22 August 1679.

Seminary priests

- Cuthbert Mayne, born at Youlston near Barnstaple, Devon, first martyr among the seminary priests; ordained at Douai, executed aged 33 at Launceston on 30 November 1577.
- John Boste, Douai, executed at Durham on 24 July 1581.
- John Paine, Douai, English College, Rome, executed at Chelmsford on 2 April 1582.
- Edmund Gennings, Douai, executed aged 24 at Grays Inn Fields on 10 December 1591.
- John Almond, Douai, English College, Rome, executed at Tyburn on 5 December 1612.
- John Plessington, Valladolid, executed aged 42 at Boughton, Chester, on 19 July 1679.

Lay men and women

- Margaret Clitherow, housewife, executed by pressing, aged 33, at York on 25 March 1582.
- Margaret Ward, domestic servant, hanged at Tyburn on 30 August 1588.
- Swithun Wells, gentleman, schoolmaster, hanged at Grays Inn Fields on 10 December 1591.
- Philip Howard, earl, died imprisoned in the Tower of London on 19 October 1595.
- Anne Line, housekeeper, hanged at Tyburn on 27 February 1601.

The martyrs of Wales

- Richard Gwyn, schoolmaster, hanged, aged 47 at Wrexham on 15 October 1584.
- John Jones, Franciscan, executed at Southwark on 12 July 1598.
- John Roberts, born at Trawsfynydd, a Benedictine, executed at Tyburn on 10 December 1610.
- John Lloyd, native of Brecon, ordained at Valladolid, executed at Cardiff on 22 July 1679.
- Philip Evans, a Jesuit, born in Monmouthshire, executed at Cardiff on 22 July 1679.
- David Lewis, a Jesuit, born at Abergavenny, executed at Usk on 27 August 1679.
- John Roberts, founder and prior of St Gregory's, Douai, executed at Tyburn on 10 December 1610.
- John Kemble, born at Rhyd-y-Car, executed at Hereford on 22 August 1679.

COPYMASTER 5 In their own words

Edmund Campion, in an Open Letter to the Government:

"The expense is reckoned, the enterprise is begun. It is of God, it cannot be withstood. So the Faith was planted, so it must be restored."

Edmund Campion, on mission, to the Jesuit General:

"I ride about some piece of the country every day. The harvest is wonderful great. On horseback I meditate my sermon; when I come to the house I polish it. Then I talk with such as come to speak with me, or hear their confessions. In the morning, after Mass, I preach; they hear with exceeding greediness and very many go to the sacraments, for the ministration whereof we are ever well assisted by the priests, whom we find in every place, whereby both the people is well served and we much eased in our charge ... There will never want in England men that will have care of their own salvation, nor such as shall advance other men's. Neither shall this Church here ever fail, so long as priest and pastors shall be found for their sheep, rage man or devil never so much."

Swithun Wells, from Newgate prison, to his brother-in-law:

"I renounced the world before ever I tasted of imprisonment, even in my baptism; which promise and profession, however slenderly soever I have kept heretofore, I purpose, for the time to come, God assisting me, to continue to my life's end."

John Wall, from prison in 1679, describing his trial:

"I was not, I thank God for it, troubled with any disturbing thoughts, for I was then of the same mind as by God's grace I ever shall be, esteeming judge and jury the best friends to me that ever I had in my life. I was so present with myself, whilst the judge pronounced sentence, that I at the same time offered myself to God ... But I told them I could not buy my own life at so dear a rate as to wrong my conscience. How God will please to dispose of all us that are condemned none know. This is the last persecution that will be in England; therefore I hope God will give all His holy grace to make the best use of it."

COPYMASTER 6 Last words

1B

John Wall, 22 August 1679, on the scaffold at Worcester:

"I will offer my life in satisfaction for my sins, and for the Catholic cause. I beseech God to bless all my benefactors and all my friends, and those that may have been in any way under my charge, and all those that suffer under this persecution; and to turn our captivity into joy; that they that sow in tears may reap in joy."

(Ms, Oscott College)

David Lewis, executed on 27 August 1679, to the crowd:

"Here is a numerous assembly — may the great Saviour of the world save every soul of you all. I believe you are here met not only to see a fellow-native die, but also to hear a dying fellow-native speak. My religion is the Roman Catholic; in it I have lived above these forty years; in it I now die, and so fixedly die, that if all the good things in this world were offered me to renounce it, all should not remove me one hair's breadth from my Roman Catholic faith.

I was condemned for reading Mass, hearing confessions, and administering the sacraments. As for reading the Mass, it was the old, and still is the accustomed and laudable liturgy of the holy Church; and all the other acts are acts of religion tending to the worship of God, and therefore dying for this I die for religion."

To his fellow Catholics:

"Friends, fear God, honour your King; be firm in your faith, avoid mortal sin by frequenting the sacraments of holy Church; bear patiently your afflictions and persecutions; forgive your enemies."

Last words:

"Sweet Jesus, receive my soul."

John Kemble was 80 when he was executed on 22 August 1679 after the Gunpowder Plot. He had worked as a priest in Wales for 54 years:

"It will be expected I should say something, but as I am an old man, it cannot be much, not having any concern in the plot, neither indeed believing there is any. Oates and Bedloe not being able to charge me with anything when I was brought up to London, though they were with me, make it evident that I die only for professing the old Roman Catholic religion, which was the religion that first made this kingdom Christian."

To the hangman, who was too upset to carry out the execution:

"Honest Anthony, my friend, Anthony, be not afraid; do thy office. I forgive thee with all my heart, thou wilt do me a greater kindness than discourtesy."

Philip Evans, executed on 22 July 1679: he was convicted after two women were persuaded to testify that he had given them Communion. While in prison awaiting execution he was treated well and even allowed to play tennis. During one game he got the news that he was to die the next day. He finished his game and then found time to play his harp and entertain visitors. He and John Lloyd were executed at Cardiff.

Final words on the scaffold:

"Sure this is the best pulpit a man can have to preach in, therefore I cannot forbear to tell you again that I die for God and religion's sake; and I think myself so happy that if I had never so many lives, I would willingly give them all for so good a cause. If I could live, it would be but for a little time, though I am but young; happy am I that can purchase with a short pain an everlasting life ... Into thy hands, O Lord, I commend my spirit."

COPYMASTER 7 Time talk

1. How far do these images and slogans reflect attitudes to time in society?

Time is money

Fast-track

Time flies

Mum, have you got time to ...

Timetable

40/40

Holiday time

Leisure time

Speed limits

All the time in the world

24/7

Time's up

Time for myself

Time out

Stop the world, I want to get off!

Quality time

I'm bored

High speed train cuts journey time in half

My job takes all my time and energy

2. With a partner, discuss some ways time affects you:
   - at home
   - at school
   - on holidays
   - with your friends and family
   - in your ambitions.

Prayers and blessings

Seasonal prayers and blessings

Lord God,
may we, your people,
who look forward to the birthday of Christ,
experience the joy of salvation
and celebrate that feast with love and thanksgiving.
(Third Sunday of Advent, C)

Father of peace,
we are joyful in your Word,
your Son Jesus Christ,
who reconciles us to you.
Let us hasten toward Easter
with the eagerness of faith and love.
(Fourth Sunday of Lent, B)

God, our Father,
let the Spirit you sent on your Church
to begin the teaching of the gospel
continue to work in the world
through the hearts of all who believe.
(Pentecost Sunday, C)

Ever-living God,
help us to celebrate our joy
in the resurrection of the Lord
and to express in our lives
the love we celebrate.
(Sixth Sunday of Easter, A)

Solemn blessings

Advent season

You believe that the Son of God once came to us, you look for him to come again.
May his coming bring you the light of his holiness and free you with his blessing.
R: Amen.
May God make you steadfast in faith, joyful in hope, and untiring in love all the days of your life.
R: Amen.
You rejoice that our Redeemer came to live with us as man.
When he comes again in glory, may he reward you with endless life.
R: Amen.

Easter season

Through the resurrection of his Son God has redeemed you and made you his children.
May he bless you with joy.
R: Amen.
The Redeemer has given you lasting freedom.
May you inherit his everlasting life.
R: Amen.
By faith you rose with him in baptism.
May your lives be holy,
so that you may be united with him for ever.
R: Amen.

COPYMASTER 9 Interview with the Epics

A B C D E **1E**

The Epics are a five-piece group from Portstown. They have just won first prize in a local radio young band of the year competition. The prize is 15 hours in a recording studio!

Int: Well done. You must be delighted with the prize?
Epics: Yeah. Thanks.
Ellie: It's what we've always wanted. It's been hard work.
Int: I bet it has. Caz, you started the band, how did it come about?
Caz: Ever since I can remember I've been into music. My family used to laugh at me singing along to Top of the Pops using my hairbrush as a mike! I got one of those junior Karaoke machines and sang along to everything.
Ellie: I think Jack and Jill was our first number!
Shauna: We were only about six!
Caz: We used to sing along to the bands and found we could do harmonies and stuff quite well.
Int: At this stage it was just you three girls, was it?
Ellie: Yes, until we started using instruments. I play drums, Caz saxophone and Shauna guitar. We felt we needed keyboards and bass for the sound we wanted, so we invited Pete and Imran to join.
Int: How did you two feel joining an all-girl band?
Imran: It was OK. We'd known each other for ages and we get on really well.
Pete: The girls are all good musicians and we like the same music. Anyway, it wasn't a 'girl band' anymore, was it?
Int: I suppose not. How much practice did it take to get to the stage you're at now?
Caz: Loads! We practised for hours every week, sometimes in Shauna's garage, sometimes in the Church Hall at weekends, and we always stay back a couple of nights after school.
Imran: That's how Jonesy first heard us.
Int: Jonesy?
Pete: Our music teacher, Mrs Jones, she was making a school CD to raise money for CAFOD.
Imran: She said we could do a couple of tracks but we had to be more … What was it?
Caz & Pete: Polished!
Imran: Yeah, that's it, polished.
Caz: We really wanted to do it. It could be our first break so we worked hard.
Ellie: Sometimes relationships got a bit tense with each other and our families.
Pete: My parents hardly saw me for weeks.
Caz: But we passed the audition, and recorded one of our own songs for the CD.
Int: How did it go down at school?
Shauna: Very well. Most people said nice things about our sound and the main thing was we raised £500 for charity.
Int: That's brilliant, but it's still a long way from young band of the year.
Caz: It is, but now we'd got the bug. It was brilliant doing the recording but the school equipment wasn't exactly top class.
Imran: Jonesy was brilliant, but she isn't exactly a professional sound engineer.
Ellie: We were determined that we wanted to record our own CD.
Caz: So we entered the competition. We had the motivation but we knew having to play 'live' for the judges would give us the push we'd need.
Pete: We were dead nervous, but when we got on stage it was fantastic.
Shauna: Yeah, it was a brilliant feeling. The nerves disappeared and we began to enjoy ourselves. It was even sweeter knowing that we'd had to work so hard for it.
Int: And the rest, as they say, is history. You will finally get to make that album. One more thing. Where did you get the name 'The Epics'?
Caz: That's a long story. I'd like to think it is made up of the initials of all our names – which of course it is … Ellie, Pete, Imran, Caz and Shauna … but the main reason is that it's an anagram of my first favourite group. See if the readers can work that one out!
Int: Well, thank you all for giving us the story of the Epics. I'm off to see if I can work out where that name really came from.

Note from the Editor: An anagram is where you rearrange the letters of one word to get another!

COPYMASTER 10 Christ will come again

Advent and Christmas proclaim the Church's belief that the coming of Jesus was part of God's plan for the world.

The readings and prayers reflect on:

(a) the message of the prophets of the Old Testament fulfilled in the historical coming of Jesus in unexpected ways

(b) hope for the future when Jesus comes again.

Work in groups.

Choose one or two Advent readings:

The Old Testament	The New Testament
Isaiah 2: 1–5	I Corinthians 1:3–9
Isaiah 11:1–10	2 Peter 3:8–14
Isaiah 40:1–5, 9–11	James 5: 7–10
Isaiah 35: 1–6, 10	Romans 16:25–27
Zephaniah 3 :14–18	Matthew 11:2–11
Micah 5: 1–4	Luke 21:25–28, 34–36
Isaiah 61:1–2, 10–11	Mark 1: 1–8

1. Identify:
   - God's promises
   - what God asks of the people
   - warnings
   - hopes
   - images that express the good things to come.

2. Share your findings.

3. Use your ICT skills to create a grid format and use it to show what these passages have to say about the coming of Jesus in history and at the end of time.

4. Use the class findings to create an Advent display, an Advent calendar or an Advent assembly for Y9.

Extension

Either: Write an essay exploring the extent to which you think the hopes of the prophets came true in Jesus.

Or: 'It will be all right in the end.' Does the promise of future hope excuse Christians from working to change the world now? Present your answer in the form of points for and against.

COPYMASTER 11 Notes for the Misereor 'Hunger Cloth'

A 'hunger cloth' is a picture bible. This is the work of an Ethiopian artist, Alemayehu Bizuneth. He uses the traditional style of his people. All the stories revolve around the central picture. Jesus is shown as the Servant of God treading the wine press, the Lamb of God who takes on himself the sin of the world. Around him are symbols of suffering and torture that call to mind victims of injustice throughout history. The 11 pictures present a 'history of salvation'. They tell of human sinfulness and God's love and mercy. Begin with the story of Cain and Able in the top left corner and continue clockwise.

I Cain and Able (Genesis 4:1–16)

In the book of Genesis, the first fratricide – the murder of brother by brother – symbolises all the prejudice and hatred that divides the human family.

Think of examples of all that causes division in families, neighbourhoods, in countries and between different groups and nations. How does the artist represent this?

II Noah (Genesis 6:9–9:17)

In the first scene people ignore the appeals of Noah and the warning storm clouds. In the second, Noah's faithfulness is rewarded and he and his family find shelter in the ark. In the third the rainbow, symbol of God's mercy, encircles the world. Think about how these Bible stories use the symbolism of darkness and light, danger and harmony to warn God's People and encourage them. Recall the rainbow parable of community (Year 7 p. 86).

III Jesus and Zacchaeus (Luke 19:1–10)

In the first scene Zacchaeus is on the outside because of his size. (And probably also because of his wealth and his dishonesty.) In scene two, Jesus calls to him.

In scene three, Zacchaeus responds to Jesus' invitation, but the bystanders are shocked. In scene four, Zacchaeus' conversion leads to action. He tells Jesus he will pay back all those he has cheated. The misereor cloth is an invitation to examine our lives. In which of the characters do I recognise myself?

IV Jesus the Compassionate (Matthew 9:35–38)

The crowds flock to Jesus. Everyone is welcome. The 'misereor' cloth takes its name from the words of Matthew, 'He was filled with pity for the crowd'. (Matthew 9:36) In Latin the words are 'misereor super turbam'. Think about different reactions to suffering: to offer to help, to feel powerless, to ignore it, to think it's not my business, to wait for others to do something.

V The feeding of the five thousand (Mark 6:30–44)

The boy is shown putting his offering into the hands of Jesus. Through him it will feed all those who are waiting. This is the cloth's message. It doesn't matter how small the offering we make. In the hands of Jesus the miracle of the multiplication of the loaves and fishes can happen again and the human family can become one at the Lord's table.

COPYMASTER 12 On death and dying

I place my hope in your promise, Lord.

(Psalm 119)

I am the resurrection.
Whoever believes in me will live,
Even though he dies;
And whoever lives and believes in me will never die.

(John 11:25–26)

We believe that Jesus died and rose again, and so we believe that God will take back with Jesus those who have died believing in him.

(1 Thessalonians 4:14)

Epitaph on a tombstone:

Remember, man, as you pass by,
as you are now, so once was I;
as I am now, so you will be,
so remember, man, eternity.

On the death of a father: a letter from a friend

Although his physical presence has gone, I know that you will continue to feel his presence and that all the small sayings that were so cheerfully expressed by him will be recalled. And there will be many times when you will be reminded of him and of his great kindness and understanding. In this way, he hasn't really died and the goodness which he spread whilst he was with us will be a support to you and all the family in the future years.

What is dying?

I am standing on the seashore. A ship sails and spreads her white sails to the morning breeze and starts for the ocean. She is an object of beauty and I stand watching her till at last she fades on the horizon, and someone at my side says, "She is gone." Gone where? Gone from my sight, that is all; she is just as large in the masts, hull and spars as she was when I saw her, and just as able to bear her load of living freight to its destination. The diminished size and total loss of sight is in me, not in her; and just at the moment when someone at my side says, "She is gone," there are others who are watching her coming, and other voices take up a glad shout, "There she comes," and that is dying.

(Bishop Brent, source unknown)

COPYMASTER 13 Prayers from the Funeral Mass

At the beginning of Mass symbols of Christian faith and life can be placed on or near the coffin.

Holy water is sprinkled in blessing, recalling Baptism.

Incense is used to honour the human body of the deceased because it will rise again.

Opening prayer

God of mercy,
you are the hope of sinners
and the joy of saints.
We pray for our brother (sister) N,
whose body we honour with Christian burial.
Give him (her) happiness with your saints,
and raise up his (her) body in glory at the last day
to be in your presence for ever.

Bidding prayers

God, the almighty Father, raised Christ his Son from the dead; with confidence we ask him to save all his people, living and dead.

For N who in baptism was given the pledge of eternal life, that he/she may now be admitted to the company of the saints.

For our brother/sister who ate the body of Christ, the bread of life, that he/she may be raised up on the last day.

For our deceased relatives and friends and for all who have helped us, that they may have the reward of their goodness.

For those who have fallen asleep in the hope of rising again, that they may see God face to face.

For the family and friends of our brother/sister N, that they may be consoled in their grief by the Lord, who wept at the death of his friend Lazarus.

For all of us assembled here to worship in faith, that we may be gathered together again in God's kingdom.

Communion Antiphon

May eternal light shine on them, O Lord, with all your saints for ever, for you are rich in mercy. Give them eternal rest, O Lord, and may perpetual light shine on them for ever, for you are rich in mercy.

1. Choose one prayer that you think would give comfort to people who have lost someone they love. Explain why.

2. Research these symbols used in a Funeral Mass and explain what they mean:
   - sign of the cross
   - holy water
   - incense.

COPYMASTER 14 Extension: I believe! We believe!

The resurrection of Jesus is really the beginning of the Church. It was such an incredible message that it is only by faith that people accept it.

The gospel of the resurrection could move people:

- to mockery
- to faith
- to murder.

Find these stories in the Acts of the Apostles:

- Acts 2:22–42
- Acts 17:32–33
- Acts 7.

Stephen was the first Christian *martyr*

Do you think he was afraid of death? Give reasons for your answer.

Martyr: witness

Throughout the history of the Church, there have been many martyrs. It takes a person of great faith to be willing to die for what he or she believes. Remember your work on the martyrs of England and Wales (1B). One of the things that many of these martyrs have in common is that they don't seem to be frightened of death. This seems to be because they believe in life after death. Their belief in the mercy of God makes death something to look forward to because it means they can share God's life more fully.

Research some men and women martyrs. The calendar of saints is a useful starting point. 'M' after a person's name means he or she died a martyr. A good one to begin with is St Lawrence, though you may not appreciate his sense of humour.

Use as your sources a liturgical calendar and dictionary of saints.

Write up notes about one martyr.

COPYMASTER 15

Model for a witness profile

A Thousand Reasons for Living

Dom Helder Camera was born into a poor family in Brazil. He was one of only four children to survive out of 14. All his life he suffered from tuberculosis. He was ordained a priest when he was 22 and by 1964 he had been appointed Archbishop. He worked among the people of the favelas (shanty towns). He encouraged them to form small groups to study the gospels. He wanted them to find life in Jesus and discover that he is the way and the truth for all people. He urged all priests and bishops to live among the poor people, like the poor Christ. When he became archbishop he put the bishop's gilded throne into storage and replaced it with a simple wooden chair. He spoke out for the poor, for the unemployed and those who were denied their rights. He founded a movement for Action, Peace and Justice and became a spokesman for the Third World.

Between 1968 and 1977 the military regime in Brazil banned him from speaking and banned anyone from naming him or quoting him. His radical approach to the cause of the poor is summed up in the most quoted of his words:

"When I give food to the poor they call me a saint, when I ask why they have no food they call me a communist."

His poems and sayings were collected in a book called A Thousand Reasons For Living. Here are some examples:

Accept surprises that upset your plans,
shatter your dreams,
give a completely different turn to your day
and – who knows? – to your life.
It is not chance.
Leave the Father free
Himself to weave the pattern of your days.

(6 July 1971)

This puffy, dirty face,
stained with sweat,
bruised by falls or blows,
belongs to some beggar or drunkard.
Or are we perhaps on Calvary
gazing at the holy face
of the Son of God?

(19 September 1971)

If you have a thousand reasons for living,
if you never feel alone,
if you wake up wanting to sing,
if everything speaks to you,
from the stone in the road
to the star in the sky,
from the loitering lizard
to the fish, lord of the sea,
if you listen to the silence,
rejoice, love walks with you,
he is your comrade, is your brother!

(28 January 1971)

Statement on behalf of Dom Helder Camera

He loved the poor like Jesus and spoke for them against the government.
He helped others to know the gospel. His prayers show he tried to find God in everyone.

COPYMASTER 16 On the sidelines

The aim of this activity is to encourage young people to reflect on where they stand when it comes to issues of injustice in the world.

(Issues you could focus on include: racism; war and peace; consumerism and fair trade; cheap labour; child workers; debt; land rights; the environment.)

Number of people: 15–30

Time: 30–40 minutes including introduction and debriefing.

Requirements:

1. A large space the size of a classroom/gym/hall (indoors or out).
2. Equipment that will help you to mark out clearly a football pitch (of course, it doesn't have to be full size). See the diagram for the important components.
3. It may be helpful to illustrate the pitch using an OHP before you actually start.
4. A Peters' projection map of the world.

Introduction

Ask the following questions:

1. Can you recall a time you were treated unfairly or unjustly? How did it feel?

   Did the story end happily or are you still left feeling sore and upset?
2. From your own experiences, can you put into words a definition of 'injustice' or do you think it will be different for everyone, depending on their situation?
3. Can you name anyone you've read about or heard about recently whom you believe to have been unfairly treated?

(Questions 4–6 might require a more in-depth discussion.)

4. Name three countries in the world where people experience injustice. Identify the injustice experienced. Identify where these countries are on a map.
5. Do you think people in the UK are concerned enough about injustice around the world?
6. Identify and make a list of the different ways in which people are informed about the world we live in.

Pitch of life

Pitch – where the action is. Involved in the issues.

Reserve bench – ready and waiting to take part in the action when called upon to do so.

Changing rooms – getting ready for action.

Terraces – shouting and supporting from the sidelines, but not really taking part in the action.

Showers – cooling off, tired from taking part in action. Needing refreshment before returning to the pitch and to the action and the issues.

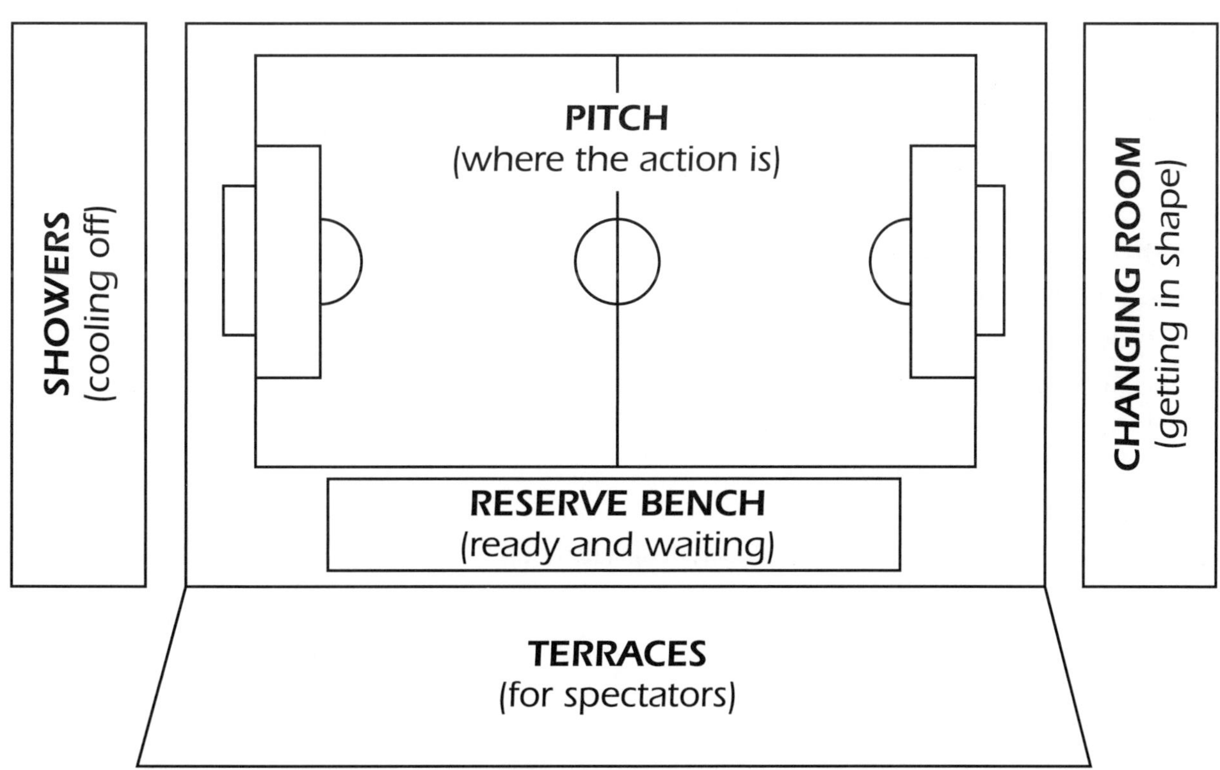

COPYMASTER 17 Prayers from the Rites of Marriage

Opening prayer

Father, you have made the bond of marriage
a holy mystery, a symbol of Christ's love for his Church.
Hear our prayers for N and N.
With faith in you and in each other,
they pledge their love today.
May their lives always bear witness to the reality of that love.

The marriage vows

I call upon these persons here present to witness
that I, N,
do take thee, N,
to be my lawful wedded wife/husband,
to have and to hold from this day forward,
for better, for worse, for richer, for poorer,
in sickness and in health,
to love and to cherish,
till death us do part.

The blessing and giving of rings

May the Lord bless these rings which you give to each other as the sign of your love and fidelity.

N, take this ring as a sign of my love and fidelity. In the name of the Father, and of the Son, and of the Holy Spirit.

From the Preface

You created man and woman out of love
and raised them to such a dignity
that in the union of husband and wife
you show us a true image of your love:
love is our origin,
love is our constant calling,
love is our fulfilment in heaven.
Thus the sacrament of marriage,
an abiding sign of your own love,
consecrates the love between husband and wife.

COPYMASTER 18 Prayers from the Rites of Ordination

1. The call

The candidates are called out from the community of believers.

Bishop: We rely on the help of the Lord God and our Saviour Jesus Christ, and we choose this man, our brother, for priesthood in the presbyteral order.

All: Thanks be to God.

In the homily the bishop encourages the candidates to be faithful to their vocation.

2. Questions and promises

To each question, the candidate replies: "I am, with the help of God."

Are you resolved, with the help of the Holy Spirit, to discharge without fail the office of priesthood in the presbyteral order as a conscientious fellow worker with the bishops in caring for the Lord's flock?

Are you resolved to celebrate the mysteries of Christ faithfully and religiously as the Church has handed them down to us for the glory of God and the sanctification of Christ's people?

Are you resolved to exercise the ministry of the word worthily and wisely, preaching the Gospel and explaining the Catholic faith?

Are you resolved to consecrate your life to God for the salvation of his people, and to unite yourself more closely every day to Christ the High priest, who offered himself for us to the Father as a perfect sacrifice?

3. Prayers for the candidates

The candidates lie prostrate during the litany of the saints. Then the bishop prays:

Hear us, Lord our God,
and pour out upon these servants of yours
the blessing of the Holy Spirit
and the grace and power of the priesthood.
In your sight we offer these men for ordination:
support them with your unfailing love.
We ask this through Christ our Lord.
All: Amen.

4. Laying on of hands

The bishop and all the priests present lay hands upon each candidate in silence. Then the bishop, with his hands extended over the candidates, prays:

Come to our help,
Lord, holy Father, almighty and eternal God;
you are the source of every honour and dignity,
of all progress and stability.
You watch over the growing human family
by your gift of wisdom and your pattern of order …
Almighty Father,
grant to this servant of yours
the dignity of the priesthood.
Renew within him the Spirit of holiness.
As a co-worker with the order of bishops,
may he be faithful to the ministry that he receives from you, Lord God,
and be to others a model of right conduct.
May he be faithful in working with the order of bishops,
so that the words of the Gospel may reach the ends of the earth,
and the family of nations,
made one in Christ,
may become God's one, holy people.

5. The priestly vestments

A priest, and members of his family, help the newly ordained to put on his priestly vestments.

6. Anointing of hands

The Father anointed our Lord Jesus Christ
through the power of the Holy Spirit.
May Jesus preserve you to sanctify the Christian people
and to offer sacrifice to God.

7. Gifts of bread and wine

Accept from the holy people of God the gifts to be offered to him.
Know what you are doing, and imitate the mystery you celebrate:
model your life on the mystery of the Lord's cross.

8. Kiss of peace

Bishop: Peace be with you.
Priest: And also with you.

Index

References in the index are to topics found in the students' book